'Thou art indeed a world, oh Rome;
and yet, were Love absent,
Then would the world be no world, then
would e'en Rome be no Rome.'

Johann Wolfgang von Goethe

LISA NIESCHLAG & LARS WENTRUP

IN LOVE WITH
ROME

Italian recipes and stories from the Eternal City

FOOD & ROME PHOTOGRAPHY

Lisa Nieschlag

ILLUSTRATION

Lars Wentrup

Hardie Grant

BOOKS

CONTENTS

LA DOLCE VITA
A STROLL THROUGH THE ETERNAL CITY

FOR AN APERITIVO
WITH FRIENDS

& STORIES

A note on oven temperatures: all ovens vary in their cooking temperatures, so you need to get to know yours, and, if necessary, use an oven thermometer. The recipes in this book have been tested in a conventional, non-fan-assisted oven at the given temperatures. If you are cooking in a fan-assisted oven, you should reduce the temperature by 10–20°C/50–60°F/2 gas marks.

CENA IN FAMIGLIA

FAMILY DINNER

LA GRANDE BELEZZA

SUNSET ON THE PIAZZA

&

STORIES

THE UNIQUE MAGIC OF ROME

As the shadows lengthen at the end of the day, young and old gather on the Pincio Terrace to watch the sun set behind the hills of the Eternal City. Although Rome seems to be coming to a halt, the air pulsates with life. In the squares, musicians play well-known melodies and snatches of Italian are mingled with languages from all over the world. There's something magical about the atmosphere.

We set off in the blazing heat, with sunhats on our heads and cameras in hand, to capture this special allure through pictures and typical Roman dishes.

We wandered aimlessly down narrow streets with bumpy cobblestones and lush bougainvillea, strolled through squares with imposing sculptures and buildings, and stopped to enjoy the view over the city from its legendary hills. We found respite on benches and at fountains, and by sipping cappuccino. We observed Romans going about their daily lives – at high speed on e-scooters or rattling Vespas, honking loudly, or hurrying through the streets on foot. We spotted many couples in love, strolling arm in arm through the city.

We got caught up in all of this and fell in love too – with Rome! With a city that lives up to its reputation as the world's largest open-air museum, where its historical significance can be felt on every corner and in every square, and where the locations featured in classic films, such as the Spanish Steps and the Trevi Fountain, are found cheek by jowl. Rome is still a vibrant city, one that is young at heart and lively well into the night. In the evening, friends and families sit in restaurants and bars on bustling piazzas, laughing or in loud discussions while eating the typical, often simple Roman dishes and drinking a glass of wine.

There we were, in the middle of it all, and we felt magically drawn to *la dolce vita*, the purely Italian way of enjoying life's pleasures that can be felt everywhere.

Lasciatevi incantare!

Lisa Nieschlag + Lars Wentrup

A STROLL THROUGH THE ETERNAL CITY

Start the day in typical Roman style with a cappuccino while standing at the counter of one of the city's numerous cafés, known as bars. After a stroll down narrow, winding streets and across history-filled squares, you can boost your energy with delicious Italian street food.

La dolce VITA

LA DOLCE VITA

Through depictions of fleeting pleasure, glamour, sex and plenty of alcohol, Federico Fellini's classic film *La Dolce Vita* (1960) paints a cynical portrait of a society in decay, bereft of values and with no future.

The handsome gossip reporter Marcello (Marcello Mastroianni) prowls through Rome's nightlife on the hunt for titillating stories about celebrities and starlets. On his forays through the bars and restaurants of the Via Veneto, he regularly succumbs to the charms of *la dolce vita* and ends up in the arms, and beds, of beautiful women. He spends a night with the rich but bored Maddalena (Anouk Aimée) in a prostitute's home. The next day he meets the famous Swedish actress Sylvia (Anita Ekberg). He falls for the unapproachable star and roams the streets of Rome with her until dawn. But Marcello doesn't find the genuine closeness and serious emotions he is looking for in his amorous adventures. The decadent and frivolous life of Roman society is as cold and empty as the desolate high-rise housing estates and the deserted streets on the outskirts of the city in which Fellini's masterpiece is partially set.

Marcello's melodramatically jealous and motherly girlfriend Emma (Yvonne Furnaux) suffers from his infidelity. She tries to persuade him to get married and have children, but Marcello feels constrained. At the same time, he admires the solid family life of his friend Steiner (Alain Cuny). He is the only person who believes in Marcello's ambitions as a writer and encourages him to finally write the book he has been planning for so long. However, when Steiner's weariness and fear of the future leads him to kill his two children and take his own life, Marcello's hopes of finding peace and quiet in a simple and peaceful life are dashed. Disillusioned and full of self-loathing, he continues his life in the superficial world of Roman party society.

As he wanders through Rome at night, Marcello meets fascinating women.

Anita Ekbert's legendary dip in the Trevi Fountain, one of the most famous scenes in film history.

13

PIZZA CON SALSICCIA

SAUSAGE PIZZA

The juicy pieces of *salsiccia*, a fresh, chunky Italian sausage, make this variety of pizza particularly tasty. It is traditionally served by the slice (*al taglio*).

MAKES 1

FOR THE DOUGH

550 g (1 lb 3 oz/4 ⅓ cups) '00' extra-fine (pastry) flour, or plain (all-purpose) flour

4 g (⅛ oz) fresh yeast or ¾ teaspoon fast-action dried (active dry) yeast

400 ml (14 fl oz/generous 1 ½ cups) lukewarm water

14 g (½ oz/2 ½ teaspoons) salt

20 ml (4 teaspoons) olive oil, plus extra for greasing

FOR THE TOPPING

200 g (7 oz/¾ cup) tinned chopped tomatoes

300 g (10 ½ oz) fresh Italian sausage

2 mozzarella balls

2 teaspoons dried oregano

2 tablespoons chilli (hot pepper) flakes

25 g (1 oz/¼ cup) freshly grated Parmesan

3 tablespoons olive oil

Salt

To make the dough, put the flour in a food processor. Dissolve the yeast in the water and gradually add while processing to form a dough. Mix to a dough for 5 minutes. Add the salt and mix for 3 more minutes. Finally, work in the oil until smooth. Transfer the dough to a bowl, cover and refrigerate for 12–24 hours.

Rest the dough at room temperature for about 2 hours. In a deep, greased baking tray (pan), use moistened hands to press and gently stretch out the dough to the edges of the tray. Cover and leave to rise in a warm place for about 1 hour.

Preheat the oven to 250°C (480°F/gas 9). Lightly salt the tomatoes for the topping. Peel the skins off the sausages. Spread the tomatoes evenly over the dough. Tear the sausages and mozzarella into pieces and spread them over the pizza. Sprinkle with oregano, chilli flakes and Parmesan. Finally, drizzle with oil and bake for about 20 minutes, until the underside of the pizza turns golden. Leave to cool slightly and cut into slices.

TIP

The dough will become lighter and more aromatic if rested for 24 hours.

PANINI CON FUNGHI, MOZZARELLA E MORTADELLA

MUSHROOM, MOZZARELLA AND MORTADELLA PANINI

One of the most famous of Rome's street foods is the mortadella panino. The locals refer to the wafer-thin mortadella slices as *mortazza*. Mortadella made with pistachios is typical of Rome. Panini are ideal as snacks for between meals, as a light lunch or to accompany an *aperitivo*, a pre-dinner drink.

Turn on a panini press or preheat the oven to 200°C (400°F/gas 6). Wipe the mushrooms clean, cut off the stalks and chop very finely with a knife or in a food processor. Tear the mozzarella into small pieces.

Heat the oil in a frying pan (skillet) and sauté the mushrooms with the oregano and rosemary until the water has evaporated and the mushrooms turn brown. Season to taste with salt and pepper.

Brush the ciabatta rolls with oil and cut in half lengthways. Spread the mushroom mixture over the two bottom halves. Arrange mortadella slices over the mushrooms and top with pieces of mozzarella. Cover with the top halves of the rolls.

Toast the panini in the panini press until golden brown. Alternatively, place the panini on a baking sheet lined with baking parchment, cover with another piece of parchment and a second baking sheet or a baking dish as a weight. Bake until the surface is crispy and the mozzarella has melted. Leave to cool briefly and enjoy.

MAKES 2

300 g (10 ½ oz) button mushrooms
1 mozzarella ball
3 tablespoons olive oil
1 teaspoon dried oregano
1 teaspoon dried rosemary
2 ciabatta rolls
75 g (2 ½ oz) mortadella with pistachio
Salt
Freshly ground black pepper

IN ADDITION

2 tablespoons olive oil, for brushing
Panini press or oven

PIZZA BIANCA CON PATATE E ROSMARINO

PIZZA BIANCA WITH POTATO AND ROSEMARY

Pizza bianca (white pizza) is pizza prepared without tomato sauce. Instead, tasty Parmesan is spread over the dough and covered with a topping of potatoes, onions and rosemary. The perfect snack to enjoy between meals.

MAKES 2

FOR THE DOUGH
4 g (⅛ oz) fresh yeast or
   ¾ teaspoon fast-action dried
   (active dry) yeast
300 ml (10 fl oz/1 ¼ cups)
   lukewarm water
500 g (1 lb 2 oz/4 cups) type
   '00' extra-fine (pastry) flour,
   or plain (all-purpose) flour,
   plus extra for dusting
10 g (½ oz/1 ¾ teaspoons) salt
10 ml (2 teaspoons) olive oil,
   plus extra for greasing

FOR THE TOPPING
250 g (9 oz) potatoes
   (preferably waxy)
3 sprigs of rosemary
½ Spanish onion
5 tablespoons olive oil
150 g (5 ½ oz/1 ¾ cups) freshly
   grated Parmesan
Salt
Fleur de sel

To make the dough, dissolve the yeast in the lukewarm water and leave overnight. Pour the mixture into a food processor or a stand mixer with a dough hook attachment, add the flour and mix for 5 minutes. Add the salt and mix for 3 more minutes. Gradually work in the oil. Halve the dough. Shape the halves into balls and place in a greased bowl, then cover and refrigerate for 12 hours.

Take the dough out of the refrigerator and leave to rise in a warm place for 1 hour. For the topping, peel the potatoes and slice very finely with a mandoline. Rinse the rosemary sprigs, pat dry, strip the leaves and mix with the potato slices. Peel and finely slice the onion, add to the potato slices with the oil and season to taste with salt. Mix the topping well.

Preheat the oven to 250°C (480°F/gas 9). On a floured work surface, stretch out the dough pieces to form pizzas of about 30 cm (12 in) in diameter, leaving the dough very thin in the centre and slightly thicker at the edges. Lay the pizzas on a sheet of baking parchment. Stretch them out a little more if necessary.

Spread 100 g (3½ oz/generous 1¼ cups) of the Parmesan on the pizzas and cover with an even layer of topping. Place the first pizza with the baking parchment on the floor of the oven and bake for 10–15 minutes, until the underside and the potatoes turn golden. Take it out and bake the second pizza. Sprinkle the finished pizzas with the remaining Parmesan and fleur de sel.

FRITTATA CON RICOTTA E ERBE AROMATICHE

FRITTATA WITH RICOTTA AND FRESH HERBS

Frittata, the Italian version of the omelette, is usually cooked and flipped over in the frying pan. This frittata has a crispy top from baking in the oven with ricotta and pecorino.

Preheat the oven to 180°C (350°F/gas 4). Peel and finely chop the shallots. Whisk the eggs with 100 g (3 ½ oz/⅓ cup) of the ricotta and the herbs until well combined. Season to taste with salt, pepper and nutmeg. Lightly season the remaining ricotta with salt.

Heat the oil in a frying pan and sauté the shallots over a medium heat until translucent. Stir the shallots into the egg mixture. Pour the mixture into the hot pan. Return the pan to the heat. Spoon the remaining ricotta over the mixture and sprinkle with the pecorino. Reduce the heat to low and allow the egg mixture to set slightly.

Then place the pan in the oven and bake the frittata for 15–18 minutes, until golden brown. Leave to cool and cut into slices. Accompany with a salad.

SERVES 2

2 shallots
6 eggs
200 g (7 oz/ generous ⅔ cup) ricotta
20 g (¾ oz/½ cup) chopped, fresh herbs (e.g. basil, oregano, thyme, olive herb)
Freshly grated nutmeg
2 tablespoons olive oil
40 g (1 ½ oz/½ cup) freshly grated pecorino
Salt
Freshly ground black pepper

IN ADDITION

Ovenproof frying pan (skillet), 24 cm (9 in) in diameter

PINSA CON MOZZARELLA DI BUFALA E RUCOLA

BUFFALO MOZZARELLA AND ROCKET PINSA

Unlike the classic pizza, pinsa is made with several types of flour and a little more water, which makes it crispy on the outside and wonderfully soft on the inside.

MAKES 4

4 g (⅛ oz) fresh yeast or ¾ teaspoon fast-action dried (active dry) yeast
330 ml (11 ¼ fl oz/1 ⅓ cups) water
400 g (14 oz/3 ¼ cups) '00' extra-fine (pastry) flour, or plain (all-purpose) flour
75 g (2 ½ oz/½ cup) rice flour, plus extra for dusting
25 g (1 oz/¼ cup) chickpea (gram) flour
10 ml (2 teaspoons) olive oil
10 g (½ oz/1 ¾ teaspoons) salt
200 g (7 oz/¾ cup) tinned chopped tomatoes
2 buffalo mozzarella balls
50 g (1 ¾ oz) rocket (arugula)
Coarse salt

IN ADDITION

Pizza stone (optional)

Dissolve the yeast in the water. Mix the yeast water with all the flours, oil and salt in a food processor for 15 minutes on a low speed setting until an elastic dough forms. Cover the dough and rest at room temperature for 1 hour, then cover and refrigerate for 12–24 hours.

Take the dough out of the refrigerator and divide into four equal pieces. Shape the pieces into balls, cover and leave to rise for about 3 hours at room temperature, until their volume has increased considerably.

Preheat the oven to 250°C (480°F/gas 9) with the pizza stone inside at the highest temperature setting for at least 30 minutes.

On a floured work surface, stretch out the dough by hand, pressing outwards from the middle to make thin pizzas with a slightly thicker crust. Top each pizza with 50 g (1 ¾ oz/3 ½ tablespoons) of the chopped tomatoes and season with salt, leaving the edges free. Using a cutting board, place each pinsa on a sheet of baking parchment and bake on the pizza stone or the floor of the oven for about 10 minutes, until the edges and the underside turn golden brown. The baking time may vary depending on the thickness of the dough and the baking temperature.

Meanwhile, tear the mozzarella into pieces. Rinse the rocket and pat dry. Top each hot pinsa with a quarter of the mozzarella ball and scatter with rocket. Drizzle with a little oil, season to taste with coarse salt and serve.

CAFFE

MARIOTTI
ICE CREAM
COFFEE

BONOMELLI

A CITY OF COFFEE AND CAPPUCCINO

A day in Rome begins and ends with a good coffee. A good espresso (*caffè*) is simply a must to round off a copious lunch or dinner. In the morning, Romans usually enjoy their coffee with a *cornetto*, their version of the croissant, while standing at the counter in one of the city's many bars. This is the only time of day when Italians drink cappuccino or another milky coffee. Every barista has a particular technique for pouring the frothed milk into the espresso, using their skills to create an artistic pattern.

MARITOZZI ALLA PANNA

ITALIAN CREAM BUNS

These soft buns filled with whipped cream are an institution in Rome. According to an old custom, future husbands would give these buns to their brides-to-be on the first Friday of March.

To make the dough, dissolve the fresh yeast in the milk and mix with the remaining ingredients in a food processor for 5 minutes, until a smooth dough forms that comes away from the sides of the bowl. Cover and leave to rise at room temperature for about 2 hours, until doubled in volume. Then deflate the risen dough and divide it into eight equal pieces.

If necessary, dust with a little flour and shape into balls, then arrange them 5 cm (2 in) apart on a baking sheet lined with baking parchment. Leave to rise in the cold oven for 30 minutes, until they have doubled in volume. This process can be assisted by placing a bowl of boiling water in the oven.

Take the tray out of the oven and preheat to 180°C (350°F/gas 4). Beat the egg with a little water. Lightly brush the buns with the egg wash and bake for about 20 minutes, until the surface turns golden brown. Leave to cool.

For the filling, whip the cream with the icing sugar to stiff peaks. Cut the maritozzi open lengthways, fill with the whipped cream and smooth the surface. Sprinkle the maritozzi with icing sugar and eat on the same day.

MAKES 8

FOR THE DOUGH

20 g (¾ oz) fresh yeast

150 ml (5 fl oz/scant ⅔ cup) full-fat (whole) milk, at room temperature

320 g (11 ¼ oz/2 ½ cups) plain (all-purpose) flour, plus extra for dusting

2 egg yolks

60 g (2 oz/4 tablespoons) unsalted butter, softened

30 g (1 oz/2 ½ tablespoons) sugar

2 tablespoons honey

6 g (¼ oz/1 teaspoon) salt

Zest of 1 organic orange

FOR THE FILLING

200 ml (7 fl oz/scant 1 cup) double (heavy) cream

75 g (2 ½ oz/⅔ cup) icing (confectioner's) sugar, plus 1 tablespoon for dusting

IN ADDITION

1 egg

29

TORTA DELLA NONNA

CUSTARD AND PINE NUT TART

A dream consisting of crispy shortcrust pastry with a vanilla custard filling and fragrant pine nuts – the kind of comfort food that only grandmothers know how to conjure up. *Dolcissima!*

SERVES 12

FOR THE SHORTCRUST PASTRY

150 g (5 ¼ oz/⅔ cup) cold butter, plus 1 tablespoon for greasing

80 g (2 ¾ oz/⅔ cup) icing (powdered) sugar

Pinch of salt

1 egg

250 g (9 oz/2 cups) '00' extra-fine (pastry) flour, plus extra for dusting

30 g (1 oz/⅓ cup) ground almonds (almond meal)

FOR THE PASTRY CREAM

½ organic lemon

750 ml (25 fl oz/3 cups) full-fat (whole) milk

1 sachet (8 g/¼ oz/2 teaspoons) vanilla sugar

200 g (7 oz/1 cup) granulated sugar

3 eggs

1 egg yolk

30 g (1 oz/¼ cup) cornflour (cornstarch)

35 g (1 ¼ oz/generous ¼ cup) plain (all-purpose) flour

IN ADDITION

50 g (1 ¾ oz/⅓ cup) pine nuts

2 tablespoons icing (powdered) sugar, for dusting

Flan dish, 24 cm (9½ in) in diameter

For the pastry, rub the butter into the icing sugar and salt until well combined and free of lumps. Briefly mix in the egg, which does not have to be fully incorporated. Mix in the flour and ground almonds to a smooth dough. Shape the dough into a ball and press flat. Wrap in cling film (plastic wrap) and refrigerate for at least 1 hour.

Meanwhile, make the pastry cream. Rinse the lemon in hot water, wipe dry and remove the zest with a vegetable peeler. Combine the milk, lemon zest, vanilla sugar and sugar in a saucepan and bring to the boil. Mix the eggs, egg yolk, cornflour and plain flour in a large bowl until smooth. When the milk comes to the boil, remove the lemon zest and add a third of the milk to the egg mixture, stirring briskly. Then pour the egg mixture into the remaining milk in the pan and bring to the boil while stirring constantly. Simmer the pastry cream for 3 minutes, transfer to a bowl and cover the surface with cling film to prevent a skin forming. Leave to cool.

Preheat the oven to 175°C (350°F/gas 4). On a floured work surface, roll out two-thirds of the pastry into a disc about 30 cm (12 in) in diameter and line a greased and dusted flan dish. Press down firmly around the sides and trim off the excess with a knife. Stir the pastry cream, pour it into the pastry case (shell) and smooth the surface. Roll out the remaining dough to a disc about 30 cm (12 in) in diameter and lay over the filling. Trim off the excess and press the edges to seal. Sprinkle the tart with pine nuts and bake for about 45 minutes, until the surface turns golden brown. Leave to cool, dust with icing sugar and serve.

AMARETTI MORBIDI CON PISTACCHI

PISTACHIO MACAROONS

These macaroons were originally made from apricot kernels. They were later replaced by sweet almonds and bitter almonds (*mandorle amare*), to which they owe the name amaretti.

Preheat the oven to 170°C (340°F/gas 3½). Finely grind the pistachios, almonds, icing sugar and vanilla sugar in a food processor. Add the egg white and mix to a smooth dough. Rest the dough for about 30 minutes.

Roll the dough into a cylinder and divide into 14–16 equal pieces. Shape each piece into a ball, roll in icing sugar and arrange, spaced a little apart, on a baking sheet lined with baking parchment. Flatten the dough balls evenly with the bottom of a glass and place a pistachio in the middle of each one. Bake for 10 minutes, until the amaretti turn golden. Leave to cool.

MAKES 14–16

60 g (2 oz/½ cup) unsalted
    pistachios, shelled
150 g (5½ oz/1 ½ cups) flaked
    (slivered) almonds
60 g (2 oz/½ cup) icing
    (powdered) sugar
½ sachet (4 g/⅛ oz/1 teaspoon)
    vanilla sugar
1 medium (US large) egg white

IN ADDITION
3 tablespoons icing
    (powdered) sugar
14–16 pistachios

BIGNÈ DI SAN GIUSEPPE

CUSTARD-FILLED CHOUX BUNS

Since the Middle Ages, Romans have celebrated the feast day of Saint Joseph (*San Giuseppe*), on 19 March, with sweet pastries. Today, you can find these creamy treats, which are deep-fried according to the traditional recipe, in every Roman bakery on this date.

MAKES 6–8

FOR THE VANILLA PASTRY CREAM

1 vanilla pod (bean), split and
   the seeds scraped out
500 ml (17 fl oz/generous
   2 cups) full-fat (whole) milk
3 egg yolks
125 g (4 ½ oz/⅔ cup) sugar
2 tablespoons cornflour
   (cornstarch)

FOR THE CHOUX PASTRY

60 g (2 oz/4 tablespoons)
   unsalted butter, softened
¼ teaspoon salt
200 ml (7 fl oz/scant 1 cup)
   water
130 g (4 ½ oz/generous 1 cup)
   plain (all-purpose) flour
3 medium (US large) eggs

IN ADDITION

Piping (pastry) bag with large
   star nozzle and small
   round nozzle
2 tablespoons icing
   (powdered) sugar

For the vanilla pastry cream, add the vanilla seeds to the milk in a saucepan and bring to the boil. Remove the pan from the heat. Whisk the egg yolks and sugar in a small bowl, sift in the cornflour and mix until smooth. Stir in a third of the milk. Add the egg and milk mixture to the remaining milk in the pan. Return the pan to the heat and gradually bring the mixture to the boil, stirring constantly, then simmer for 2–3 minutes to a creamy consistency. Transfer the pastry cream to a plastic bowl and immediately cover the surface with cling film (plastic wrap) to prevent a skin from forming. Leave to cool and refrigerate for at least 2 hours.

Preheat the oven to 220°C (425°F/gas 7). Combine the butter, salt and water in a saucepan and bring to the boil. When the butter has melted, add the flour. Stir vigorously with a wooden spoon until the mixture clumps and a white film has formed on the bottom of the pan. Transfer the resulting paste, or panade, to a bowl and leave to cool. Add in the eggs one at a time, stirring vigorously to a smooth batter.

Transfer the choux pastry to a piping bag fitted with a large star nozzle and pipe six to eight rosettes on a baking sheet lined with baking parchment. Place a small ovenproof dish filled with water in the bottom of the oven. Place the tray with the choux puffs on the second oven shelf and bake for 30–35 minutes. Remove from the oven and leave to cool.

Transfer the pastry cream to a piping bag fitted with a small round nozzle and fill the choux buns. Top the choux buns with a little pastry cream. Finally, dust with icing sugar.

CROSTATA CON CASSIS

ITALIAN BLACKBERRY JAM TART

As early as the 15th century, Italian *pasticciere* were devising tarts with crispy pastry cases (shells) and sweet fruit fillings, which became known as *crostate*. Romans still love a good crostata today. The shortcrust pastry is usually filled with fruit, such as blackcurrants, or ricotta cheese.

To make the pastry, rub the butter into the icing sugar and salt in a food processor or by hand until well combined and free of lumps. Incorporate the egg. Mix in the flour and ground almonds to a smooth dough. Shape the dough into a ball and press flat. Wrap in cling film (plastic wrap) and refrigerate for at least 1 hour.

Preheat a fan (convection) oven to 175°C (375°F/gas 5). On a floured work surface, roll out the dough to a thickness of about 5 mm (¼ in), line the greased and dusted flan tin and press down firmly. Trim off any excess if necessary. Roll out the remaining dough into a circle and use a pizza cutter to cut into strips about 2 cm (¾ in) wide. Alternatively, you can cut out other shapes.

Stir the jam until smooth and spread it over the pastry in the tin. Arrange the pastry strips in a lattice pattern over the filling. Bake for 35 minutes, until the surface turns golden brown. Leave to cool in the tin, then remove and dust with icing sugar.

SERVES 12

FOR THE SHORTCRUST PASTRY
150 g (5 ½ oz/⅔ cup) cold butter, plus extra for greasing
80 g (2 ¾ oz/⅔ cup) icing (powdered) sugar, plus extra for dusting
Pinch of salt
1 egg
250 g (9 oz/2 cups) '00' extra-fine (pastry) flour, plus extra for dusting
30 g (1 oz/⅓ cup) ground almonds (almond meal)

IN ADDITION
400–500 g (14 oz–1 lb 2 oz/1 ¼–1 ½ cups) blackcurrant jam (preserve)
Flan tin (tart pan; 24 cm/9 ½ in diameter)

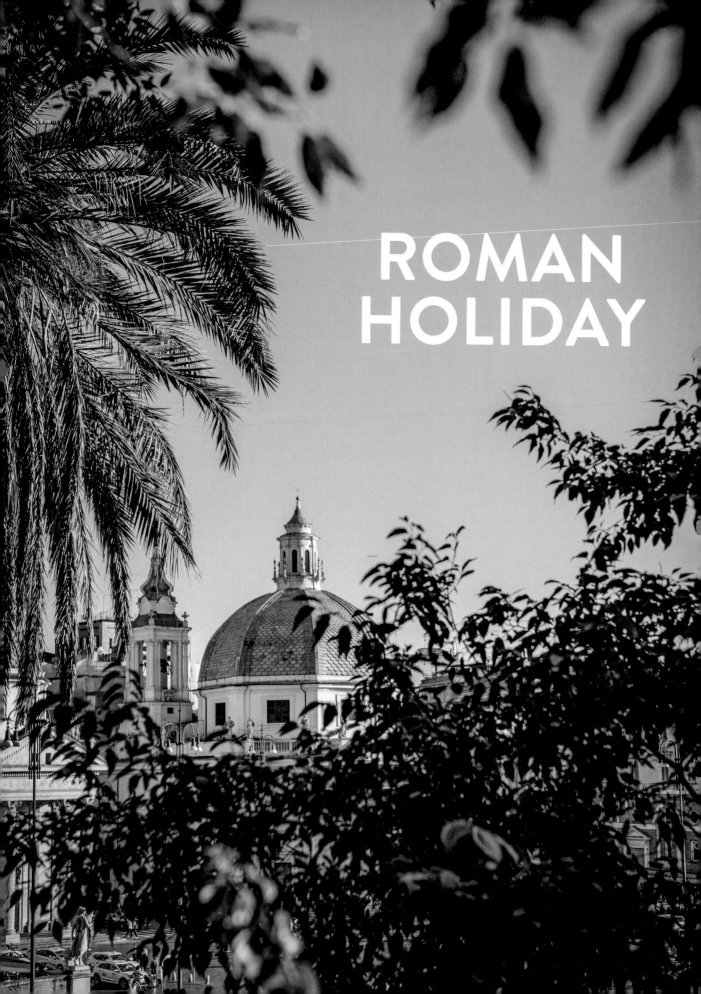

ROMAN HOLIDAY

'Rome. By all means, Rome. I will cherish my visit here in memory as long as I live,' replies Princess Ann (Audrey Hepburn) at the end of the romantic comedy *Roman Holiday* (1953) when asked by a journalist which city she enjoyed the most on her tour of Europe. The reason for her enthusiasm for the Eternal City is love, of course, and the man with whom she could forget her official duties for a day and enjoy her freedom in the bustling metropolis.

The previous day, Princess Ann escaped from the rigid court protocol with the intention of exploring Rome anonymously on her own and doing whatever she wanted for a day. She meets the American reporter Joe Bradley (Gregory Peck), who senses a sensational story. He pretends not to recognise Ann and shows her around the

city. Director William Wyler takes us on a wonderful sightseeing tour through Rome in the 1950s. The two meet for the first time at the Roman Forum. Ann gets a fashionable short hairstyle at a barber shop by the Trevi Fountain and eats a gelato on the Spanish Steps. Joe invites her for a glass of champagne at Café G. Rocca in Via della Rotonda, by the Pantheon, where they are joined by his friend, Irving – a photographer who is supposed to take secret, candid pictures for Joe's exclusive story. Joe and Ann then wander through the streets on the back of a Vespa, past the Colosseum and across the lively Piazza Venezia. Finally, they stand before the Bocca della Verità, the mouth of truth that will bite off the hand of every liar. The day ends with an evening of dancing on the Tiber by Castel Sant'Angelo. But the secret police are already on Ann's trail, and it all comes to a head with a brawl and the two protagonists jumping into the river.

At the end of the day, Ann and Joe discover that they have fallen in love with each other. Nonetheless, Ann returns to her old life. When they see each other the next day at the press reception, they know that it will be the last time. Joe tells Ann that she can trust him and that he won't write the story.

BOMBOLONI AL CIOCCOLATO

ITALIAN DOUGHNUTS WITH CHOCOLATE SAUCE

Bomboloni are very popular in Italy. These balls of yeasted dough are typically filled with pastry cream or chocolate. They also make a visually appealing dessert when drizzled with chocolate sauce.

MAKES 24–26

FOR THE DOUGH

8 g (¼ oz) fresh yeast or 1 ½ teaspoons fast-action dried (active dry) yeast

200 ml (7 fl oz/scant 1 cup) lukewarm water

300 g (10 ½ oz/generous 2 ⅓ cups) '00' extra-fine (pastry) flour

5 g (¼ oz/scant 1 teaspoon) salt

1 teaspoon sugar

IN ADDITION

1 litre (34 fl oz/4 ¼ cups) refined rapeseed (canola) oil or groundnut (peanut) oil

100–150 g (3½–5½ oz/½–¾ cup) chocolate-hazelnut spread

Dissolve the yeast in the lukewarm water. Combine the yeast water with the flour, salt and sugar, but without mixing too vigorously or the dough will become tough. Cover the dough and leave to rise in a warm place for 45 minutes or until it doubles in volume.

Heat the oil in a small saucepan to 170°C (340°F). Scoop out the dough with a tablespoon and use a second spoon to shape it into walnut-size balls. Then fry in the hot oil until golden brown. Only fry three or four balls at a time. Drain on some kitchen paper (paper towel) and leave to cool.

Heat the chocolate-hazelnut spread in the microwave until runny, then drizzle over the bomboloni.

AFFOGATO AL CAFFÈ

AFFOGATO

A scoop of vanilla ice cream drowned (*affogato*) in hot espresso makes the perfect coffee treat for a warm summer's evening on the terrace of a café on the Piazza Navona. Enjoy it like the Romans do, by eating the ice cream with a small spoon and drinking the espresso.

Combine the cream with the vanilla seeds in a saucepan and bring to the boil. Remove from the heat and transfer to a bowl. Leave to cool in the refrigerator. Whip the vanilla-infused cream to stiff peaks and fold into the condensed milk. Transfer the mixture to a freezer-safe, airtight container, cover with the lid and freeze for at least 4 hours.

Place two scoops of ice cream in a glass or cup and pour hot espresso over the top. Add a shot of Amaretto (if using).

MAKES 2

FOR THE VANILLA ICE CREAM
500 ml (17 fl oz/generous 2 cups) double (heavy) cream
1 vanilla pod (bean), split and the seeds scraped out
400 g (14 oz) tin condensed milk

IN ADDITION
4 shots espresso
1 shot Amaretto (optional)
Ice cream scoop

FOR AN
APERITIVO
WITH
FRIENDS

Romans like to mark the end of the day with a drink before dinner, known as *aperitivo*. It is usually accompanied by finger foods such as nuts, olives or bruschetta. What could be better than drinking a toast to life in delightful company?

Il dolce far niente

THE PLEASURE OF DOING NOTHING

THE ROMANS AND THEIR ATTITUDE TO LIFE

When it comes to finding pleasure in idleness, Italians are the masters. And Rome is the perfect place to celebrate the Italian lifestyle. What could be more relaxing than strolling through the narrow streets of the old city, enjoying an espresso in a café while watching the rich tapestry of life unfolding in the streets, or taking in the magnificent view over the Eternal City from one of its hills? Time moves more slowly in Rome, and the Romans have mastered the art of forgetting the time, even amid the hustle and bustle of the big city, and enjoying the moment with good food, a glass of wine and stimulating conversation.

BRUSCHETTE CALDE

BRUSCHETTE WITH TOMATO CONFIT

In the early evening, people meet for an *aperitivo* in a bar or restaurant in Rome. All kinds of delicacies, such as *bruschette*, olives, bread and salads, are usually included in the price of the drink.

MAKES 4

800 g (1¾ lb/5 ⅓ cups) cherry
  tomatoes
5 garlic cloves
100 ml (3½ fl oz/scant ½ cup)
  olive oil
1 ciabatta loaf
4 sprigs of basil
Coarse sea salt
Salt
Freshly ground black pepper

IN ADDITION

Ovenproof dish or casserole
  dish (Dutch oven)

Preheat the oven to 200°C (400°F/gas 6). Wash the tomatoes and remove the stalks. Peel the garlic cloves. Put the tomatoes in an ovenproof dish or casserole dish (Dutch oven) with the whole garlic cloves and 80 ml (2¾ fl oz/⅓ cup) of oil, season to taste with salt and pepper, and bake for 20 minutes, stirring halfway through.

Cut the bread into slices, 1.5–2 cm (½–¾ in) thick. Drizzle one side at a time with the remaining oil. Toast the slices in the oven for 10 minutes.

Wash the basil, shake dry and pluck the leaves. Remove the tomatoes from the oven, gently press and then spread them over the toasted ciabatta slices. Drizzle over the bruschette with half the cooking liquid and serve sprinkled with basil leaves and sea salt.

CALAMARI FRITTI CON SALSA DI AGLIO

DEEP-FRIED CALAMARI WITH GARLIC DIP

Served as an antipasto with a savoury dip and as a main course in Roman restaurants, these deep-fried squid rings symbolise the Mediterranean lifestyle.

To make the batter, mix the flour with some salt and pepper to taste and the paprika. Stir in the olive oil. Gradually stir in the water until the batter is smooth. Refrigerate for at least 1 hour.

Heat the rapeseed oil in a deep saucepan to 175°C (350°F). The oil is hot enough when you dip a wooden spoon into it and bubbles form at the tip. Rinse the squid rings and pat dry, then season with salt and dredge in the flour. Dip the rings fully into the batter, then remove, briefly drain the excess and deep-fry in the hot oil. Drain on kitchen paper (paper towels). Drizzle with a little lemon juice before serving.

For the dip, whisk the olive oil and egg yolk (use a very fresh egg) in a blender beaker using a hand-held blender to a creamy mayonnaise.

Peel the garlic and crush in a garlic press. Stir the garlic, mustard and lemon juice into the mayonnaise and season to taste with salt.

SERVES 4

FOR THE CALAMARI

240 g (8 ½ oz/scant 2 cups) plain (all-purpose) flour, plus extra for dredging

1 teaspoon sweet paprika

180 ml (6 fl oz/¾ cup) olive oil

360 ml (12 fl oz/1 ½ cups) ice-cold water

1.2 kg (2 lb 10 ½ oz) squid rings (pre-cut and ready to cook)

A little lemon juice

Salt

Freshly ground black pepper

FOR THE DIP

150 ml (5 fl oz/scant ⅔ cup) olive oil

1 egg yolk

3 garlic cloves

½ teaspoon medium-strength mustard

1 dash of fresh lemon juice

Salt

IN ADDITION

1 litre (34 fl oz/4 ¼ cups) refined rapeseed (canola) oil

SUPPLÌ

DEEP-FRIED RICE BALLS

These deep-fried rice balls, which are available in countless varieties and throughout the city, should be sampled by travellers to Rome at least once. *Supplì* filled with ragù (minced meat sauce) and mozzarella are a Roman staple.

MAKES 20

1 Spanish onion

1 carrot

4 tablespoons olive oil

200 g (7 oz) minced (ground) beef

4 tablespoons tomato purée (paste)

120 ml (4 fl oz/½ cup) white wine

500 ml (17 fl oz/generous 2 cups) beef stock

300 g (10 ½ oz/1 ¼ cups) tomato passata (sieved tomatoes)

200 g (7 oz/1 cup) risotto rice

80 g (2 ¾ oz/1 cup) freshly grated pecorino

3 eggs

250 g (9 oz) mozzarella

Salt

Freshly ground black pepper

IN ADDITION

Plain (all-purpose) flour, for dredging

100 g (3 ½ oz/1 cup) dried breadcrumbs

1 litre (34 fl oz/4 ¼ cups) refined rapeseed (canola) oil or groundnut (peanut) oil

Peel and finely chop the onion and carrot and sauté in a large frying pan (skillet) with 2 tablespoons of olive oil. Add the beef and tomato purée and sauté until the meat browns. Pour in the white wine and allow to evaporate.

In a saucepan, combine the stock with the passata and bring to the boil. Transfer the contents of the frying pan to a bowl. Heat the remaining 2 tablespoons of olive oil in the pan and sauté the rice. Deglaze with a little of the hot tomato and stock mixture. As soon as the rice absorbs the liquid, add a little more, then repeat the process until the rice is al dente, or slightly undercooked. Add the rice to the meat, mix and leave to cool. Stir in the pecorino and 1 egg. Season to taste with salt and pepper.

Beat the remaining 2 eggs in a bowl and season with salt and pepper. Put the flour in a second bowl and the breadcrumbs in a third. Tear the mozzarella into small pieces. Shape the rice and beef mixture into apricot-size balls, press a hole in each and insert a piece of mozzarella.

Heat the rapeseed or groundnut oil in a saucepan to 170°C (340°F). The oil is hot enough when you dip a wooden spoon into it and bubbles form at the tip. Dredge the balls one at a time in the flour and coat in egg and breadcrumbs. Fry three supplì at a time until golden brown.

Drain on some kitchen paper (paper towels) and serve hot.

FILETTI DI BACCALÀ

BATTERED COD FILLETS

Tender fish fillets fried in crispy beer batter are a Roman speciality, although the dish actually has Jewish origins. Rome is home to one of the oldest Jewish communities in Europe.

Rinse the cod fillets, pat dry and cut into bite-size pieces. Season to taste with salt on both sides and dredge in a little flour.

Mix the flour with the baking powder. Mix the egg with the beer and water and season with salt and pepper. Then stir the egg mixture into the flour to a smooth batter.

Heat the oil in a pot to 175°C (350°F). The oil is hot enough when you dip a wooden spoon into it and bubbles form at the tip. One at a time, dip the cod pieces into the batter and fry in the hot oil until golden brown. Do not fry more than three or four pieces at a time, otherwise the temperature of the oil will drop. Drain on kitchen paper (paper towels) and serve hot with a lemon wedge.

TIP
A herb dip makes an ideal accompaniment.

SERVES 4

1.2 kg (2 lb 10 ½ oz) cod fillets
250 g (9 oz/2 cups) plain (all-purpose) flour, plus extra for dredging
1 teaspoon baking powder
1 medium (US large) egg
180 ml (6 fl oz/¾ cup) cold beer
300 ml (10 fl oz/1 ¼ cups) cold water
Salt
Freshly ground black pepper

IN ADDITION
1 litre (34 fl oz/4¼ cups) refined rapeseed (canola) oil or groundnut (peanut) oil
1 lemon

PANE

Pane, prosciutto e parmigiano – simple culinary delights of the highest quality are literally waiting on the next street corner in Rome. You can buy fine Parma ham and San Daniele prosciutto at a *salumeria*, which is often more of a delicatessen than simply a shop selling charcuterie, and different fine cheeses are also on offer. Many Roman bakeries (*panifici*) not only have a large selection of bread and sweet pastries, but also make pizza. It is baked in the form of long sheets in a wood-fired oven (*antico forno*) and sold *al taglio* to take away. At some long-established specialist pizza bakeries, you can enjoy your freshly made pizza at small bar tables inside the shop.

PROSCIUTTO

OLIVE ALL'ASCOLANA

DEEP-FRIED OLIVES STUFFED WITH MINCED BEEF

The original recipe uses the Ascolana Tenera variety of olives, large and soft olives that are easy to fill with minced meat. They are native to the Ascoli Piceno region to which they owe their name.

MAKES 4 SERVINGS OR 40 PIECES

3 tablespoons olive oil
200 g (7 oz) minced (ground)
   beef
1 tablespoon tomato purée
   (paste)
50 ml (1 ¾ fl oz/3 ½ tablespoons)
   white wine
30 g (1 oz/⅓ cup) freshly grated
   Parmesan
400 g (14 oz/2 ⅔ cups) large
   green olives, pitted
Salt
Freshly ground black pepper

IN ADDITION

1 litre (34 fl oz/4 ¼ cups) refined
   rapeseed (canola) oil
   or groundnut (peanut) oil
2 eggs
Plain (all-purpose) flour,
   for dredging
100 g (3 ½ oz/1 cup) dried
   breadcrumbs

Heat the oil in a frying pan (skillet) and brown the minced beef together with the tomato purée. Deglaze with the white wine and reduce the liquid.

Transfer the contents of the frying pan to a bowl, leave to cool slightly and season to taste with salt and pepper. Stir in the Parmesan and then process the mixture with a hand-held blender. Cut open the sides of the olives and fill them with the meat mixture.

Heat the oil in a saucepan to 170°C (340°F). The oil is hot enough when you dip a wooden spoon into it and bubbles form at the tip. Beat the eggs in a small bowl and season with salt and pepper. Put the flour in a second bowl and the breadcrumbs in a third. Dredge the stuffed olives one at a time in the flour and coat in egg and breadcrumbs, then deep-fry in hot oil. Drain on kitchen paper (paper towels) and serve lukewarm.

CONCIA DI ZUCCHINE

FRIED COURGETTES MARINATED WITH VINEGAR AND MINT

A large number of Roman culinary specialities can be traced back to the influence of traditional Jewish cuisine, including these marinated courgettes with mint. The traditional recipe uses the Zucchina Romanescha variety, which is recognised by its pale stripes.

Halve and thinly slice the courgettes. Lightly season with salt, leave to rest in a bowl for 10 minutes and then carefully pat dry with kitchen paper (paper towels). Rinse the mint, pat dry, pluck the leaves and cut into fine strips.

Heat the oil in a frying pan (skillet) and fry the courgette slices a few at a time until golden brown. Drain on kitchen paper. Arrange on a plate, drizzle with the vinegar and garnish with mint. They can be enjoyed hot or cold.

SERVES 4

2 medium courgettes (zucchini)
2 sprigs of mint
150 ml (5 fl oz/scant ⅔ cup) olive oil
3 tablespoons white wine vinegar
Salt

INVOLTINI DI MELANZANE

STUFFED AUBERGINE ROLLS
WITH TOMATO SAUCE

In this irresistible classic, aubergine rolls are filled with a rich mascarpone and ricotta cream and baked in the oven. A quick and easy dish for a warm summer's evening.

<u>SERVES 4</u>

3 small aubergines (eggplants)
3 garlic cloves
3 tablespoons olive oil
400 g (14 oz/1 ⅔ cups) tinned
   chopped tomatoes
1 sprig of basil
100 g (3 ½ oz/scant ½ cup)
   mascarpone
100 g (3 ½ oz/generous ⅓ cup)
   ricotta
25 g (1 oz/¼ cup) freshly grated
   Parmesan
1 egg yolk
1 mozzarella ball
Salt
Freshly ground black pepper

<u>IN ADDITION</u>
Ovenproof dish or casserole
   dish (Dutch oven)
1 ciabatta loaf

Preheat the oven to 190°C (375°F/gas 5). Trim the tops from the aubergines and slice lengthways as thinly as possible, making sure there are no holes. Season to taste with salt and fry a few at a time in a dry non-stick frying pan (skillet). Leave to cool.

Peel and finely chop the garlic. Heat the oil in a saucepan and sauté the garlic over a low heat. Add the tomatoes and season with salt. Put the tomato sauce in an ovenproof dish or casserole.

For the filling, rinse the basil, pat dry, pluck the leaves and cut into thin strips. In a bowl, mix the mascarpone, ricotta and Parmesan with the basil and egg yolk. Season with salt and pepper.

Spread 1 tablespoon of filling over each aubergine slice, roll into small parcels and place in the tomato sauce. Tear the mozzarella into small pieces and spread over the parcels. Bake the *involtini* for 35 minutes until the cheese turns golden brown. Serve warm with the ciabatta.

ASPARAGI DI PESTO CON PROSCIUTTO DI PARMA

ASPARAGUS WITH PESTO AND PARMA HAM

There are hundreds of ways to enjoy Parma ham. One of the finest combinations is with green asparagus, pine nuts, Parmesan and pesto. A pleasure, and not only for the palate.

Wash the basil, shake dry and pluck the leaves. Peel the garlic and purée together with the basil, pine nuts and oil using a hand-held blender. Stir in the grated Parmesan and season the pesto to taste with salt and pepper.

Wash the asparagus and trim off a good portion of the ends. Heat the oil in a large frying pan (skillet) and sauté the asparagus over a medium heat. When the asparagus has taken on some colour, add a little water and cover the pan with a lid. Steam the asparagus for 5 minutes until al dente.

Toast the pine nuts in a dry frying pan until fragrant. To serve, arrange the asparagus on plates and drizzle with 70 g (2½ oz/¼ cup) of pesto. Top with Parma ham and scatter with Parmesan shavings and the toasted pine nuts. Ciabatta makes a good accompaniment.

TIP

You can store the leftover pesto in a screw-top jar in the refrigerator.

SERVES 4

FOR THE PESTO

100 g (3½ oz/3⅓ cups) fresh basil
    leaves
1 garlic clove
30 g (1 oz/¼ cup) pine nuts
100 ml (3½ fl oz/scant ½ cup)
    olive oil
20 g (¾ oz/¼ cup) freshly grated
    Parmesan
Salt
Freshly ground
    black pepper

FOR THE ASPARAGUS

800 g (1 lb 12 oz) green
    asparagus spears
1 tablespoon olive oil

IN ADDITION

20 g (¾ oz/2½ tablespoons)
    pine nuts
150 g (5½ oz) Parma ham
    (Prosciutto di Parma)
50 g (1¾ oz/½ cup) Parmesan
    shavings

BATHED IN WARM EVENING LIGHT

On sunny and hot summer days in Rome, the early evening hours are an invitation to escape the commotion and noise with a walk under the shade of the trees. On the city's many hills, you can enjoy the tranquillity of the greenery as well as splendid views over the rooftops of the Eternal City, which the setting sun bathes in an atmospheric evening light.

CARCIOFI ALLA ROMANA

ROMAN-STYLE ARTICHOKES

This is a typical dish of the Lazio region, for which the large purple Carciofo Romanesco variety of artichoke is traditionally used. Slow steaming transforms the vegetable, with its garlic and mint filling, into an aromatic side dish or starter (appetiser).

SERVES 4

8 artichokes
juice of 1 lemon
20 g (¾ oz/⅔ cup) mint
40 g (1 ½ oz/2 cups) parsley
2 garlic cloves
Salt
Freshly ground black pepper

IN ADDITION

100 ml (3½ fl oz/scant ½ cup)
    olive oil

Trim the artichokes by cutting the stalk in half and removing the tough outer leaves. Then cut off the top half of the artichokes and make sure there are no hard parts left. Place the cleaned artichokes in a bowl with some water and the lemon juice.

Rinse the mint and parsley, pat dry and pluck and finely chop the leaves. Peel the garlic cloves, chop very finely and mix with the herbs. Season the mixture to taste with salt and pepper and carefully stuff the artichokes with the filling. Prise the inner leaves apart if necessary.

Heat the oil in a pot. Place the artichokes cut-side down inside the pot. Add 250 ml (8 fl oz/1 cup) water, cover the pot with a lid and cook for 45 minutes. The artichokes can be enjoyed cold as an antipasto or hot as an accompaniment for savoury dishes.

PASTA E FAGIOLI

PASTA AND BEAN SOUP

This rustic dish brings back childhood memories of being in grandmother's kitchen. Smoked bacon gives a savoury note to this *piatto della nonna*, timeless comfort food made by grandmothers, which is ideal for a cool evening on the piazza.

Soak the beans overnight in cold water to soften. The following day, cook in unsalted water for 1 hour. Meanwhile, peel and finely chop the carrot, onion, celeriac and garlic.

Heat the olive oil in a pot and sauté the vegetables and bacon over a low heat, stirring until lightly coloured. Add the water, followed by the passata. Cover and simmer over a medium heat for 30 minutes.

Cook the pasta according to the packet instructions until al dente. Then pour off the water, leave to drain briefly and add to the soup. Wash the spinach and add to the soup together with the beans. Season to taste with salt and pepper. Add chilli flakes if using. Serve the soup in bowls drizzled with oil.

SERVES 4

100 g (3½ oz/½ cup) dried borlotti (cranberry) beans, or cannellini beans

1 carrot

1 Spanish onion

¼ celeriac (celery root)

2 garlic cloves

25 ml (5 teaspoons) olive oil, plus extra for serving

125 g (4 ½ oz) smoked bacon, cubed

1.5 litres (51 fl oz/6⅓ cups) water

200 g (7 oz/¾ cup) tomato passata (sieved tomatoes)

200 g (7 oz/2 cups) pasta (e.g. orecchiette or pipe rigate)

100 g (3½ oz/3 ½ cups) spinach leaves

Chilli (hot pepper) flakes (optional)

Salt

Freshly ground black pepper

ALBICOCCHE GRATINATE CON CREMA DI RICOTTA

GRILLED APRICOTS WITH RICOTTA CREAM

These caramelised apricots served lukewarm on a bed of luscious ricotta cream are a heavenly treat.

SERVES 4

FOR THE APRICOTS
1 kg (2 lb 4 oz) ripe apricots
125 g (4 ½ oz/⅔ cup) sugar
1 vanilla pod (bean), split and
    the seeds scraped out

FOR THE PASTRY CREAM
250 g (9 oz/1 cup) cold ricotta
200 g (7 oz/generous ¾ cup)
    double (heavy) cream
50 g (1 ¾ oz/generous ⅓ cup)
    icing (powdered) sugar

IN ADDITION
4 tablespoons olive oil

Halve and stone (pit) the apricots and mix in a bowl with the sugar, vanilla seeds and vanilla pod. Marinate for 30 minutes. Meanwhile, preheat the oven to 220°C (425°F/gas 7). Remove the vanilla pod, transfer the apricots to an ovenproof dish and roast in the oven for 20 minutes.

For the ricotta cream, whisk all the ingredients in a bowl until fluffy, then refrigerate.

Remove the apricots from the oven; they should be slightly caramelised and soft. Leave to cool a little. Divide the cream among four shallow bowls. Arrange the apricots on top of the cream and drizzle 1 teaspoon of olive oil over each bowl. Serve immediately while the apricots are still slightly warm, otherwise the cream will collapse.

THE ETERNAL CITY

THE WORLD'S LARGEST OPEN-AIR MUSEUM

Although legend has it that Rome was founded by Romulus and Remus – who were raised by a she-wolf – in 753 BC, the city's history can actually be traced back over 3,000 years. It is no wonder then that the poet Tibullus, as early as the first century BC, described the metropolis on the Tiber as the 'Eternal City'. By that time, the Roman Forum – with its temples, market complexes and triumphal arches, and the centre of political, economic, cultural and religious life in antiquity – was already bursting at the seams. By the first century AD, Rome already had one million inhabitants.

In no other city in the world are monuments and art treasures from so many different eras crammed into such a small space as in Rome. Anyone visiting the Eternal City for the first time and strolling through the city centre on a sightseeing tour will be overwhelmed by the abundance of world-famous reminders of times long past that can be found on almost every street corner. You can still cross the Tiber today on bridges built in Roman times. Ancient buildings, such as the Colosseum, characterise the cityscape, as do numerous Baroque fountains.

GRANITA DI ANGURIA

WATERMELON GRANITA

Although originating in Sicily, sweet watermelon granita is just the thing to round off a summer's day in the Eternal City. It can be served either as a dessert or a cold beverage.

SERVES 4

600 g (1 lb 5 oz) watermelon,
skin and seeds removed
(4 cups diced)
2 sprigs of basil
120 g (4 ¼ oz/1 cup) icing
(powdered) sugar
200 ml (7 fl oz/scant 1 cup) rosé

Cut the flesh of the watermelon into large chunks.
Wash the basil, shake dry and pluck the leaves.

Place all the ingredients in a blending beaker and purée finely with a hand-held blender. Transfer the mixture to a freezer-safe container, cover with the lid and freeze for at least 6 hours.

Scrape the granita with a fork and serve in bowls or glasses.

TIP
You can top the granita with rosé and
serve it as a refreshing cocktail.

AMERICANO

According to legend, the Americano cocktail was created in the
1860s as a mixture of Campari and red vermouth (Cinzano). Its low
alcohol content makes this bittersweet classic the ideal cocktail for an
afternoon of *la dolce vita*.

MAKES 4

1 organic orange
Juice of 1 pink grapefruit
200 ml (7 fl oz/scant 1 cup)
Italian bitter liqueur
200 ml (7 fl oz/scant 1 cup)
sweet red vermouth
Ice cubes

Wash the orange in hot water, pat dry and shave off the zest with a
vegetable peeler. Mix the grapefruit juice with the bitter liqueur and
vermouth. Fill four glasses with ice cubes and fill with the cocktail.
Garnish with a twist of orange zest.

LIMONCELLO & TONIC

'Know'st thou the land where lemon trees do bloom?' (Goethe). It would be hard to find a fruit with such a strong association with Italy as the lemon. It is at its most delicious when served as ice-cold limoncello. And with the addition of sparkling tonic water, it becomes the perfect summer drink.

MAKES 4

½ organic lemon
160 ml (5 ½ fl oz/⅔ cup)
limoncello (lemon liqueur)
Ice cubes
4 sprigs of basil
800 ml (27 fl oz/3 ⅓ cups)
strong tonic water

Rinse the lemon in hot water, pat dry and cut into thin slices. Divide the limoncello among four glasses and add ice cubes. Fill each glass with 200 ml (7 fl oz/scant 1 cup) of tonic water. Place 1 lemon slice in each glass. Garnish each cocktail with a sprig of basil.

FAMILY DINNER

Cena in FAMIGLIA

Good food and family come first in Italy. When everyone gathers around the dinner table, they philosophise about life, laugh or have heated discussions. There are also traditional *piatti di nonna – delizioso!*

GOOD FOLK'S
Sunday

A Sunday like any other. Rome awakens. The wooden shutters are opened and the sounds of the city enter people's homes. The classic Italian neorealist film, *La domenica della buona gente*, released in English as *Good Folk's Sunday* (1953), is all about the little people. It features individual stories about dashed hopes, shattered dreams, quarrels and reconciliation, love and revenge. They are all skilfully intertwined and culminate at a stadium where the Roman football (soccer) team Roma is playing against Napoli that Sunday.

Former footballer Bruno Pieri hopes to find a job as a trainer for the team from Naples, which will allow him to solve his marital problems. At the same time, a family man believes he has won a lot of money by betting on the match results and makes big plans, but he gets upset when he realises he has missed out. The beautiful Sandra (Maria Fiore) wants to introduce her fiancé, the unemployed Giulio (Renato Salvatori), to her uncle, who is supposed to find him a job. Ines (Sophia Loren) is travelling by train from Salerno. She is looking for her lover, the successful lawyer Luigi Conti (Vittorio Sanipoli), who has abandoned her, despite getting her pregnant. Luigi, however, has been ignoring her. So Ines, who has come to Rome with a pistol in her handbag and clear intentions, hopes to meet him at the stadium.

Ines meets Giulio outside the stadium. He has stood up Sandra and her uncle because he would rather watch the

football match with his friends, but he can't afford a ticket. Ines pays for his ticket. The two go into the stadium together and Giulio manages to calm Ines down. When Sandra sees Giulio in the stadium with the other woman, she gets angry.

Ines meets Luigi at the railway station before her departure. When she tries to take revenge, she realises that her gun is missing. It turns out that Giulio had discovered the gun and had taken it out of her bag. Disappointed, Ines leaves. Meanwhile, Sandra makes a scene in front of Giulio's friends. By now it's evening. The two argue in the streets of Rome. Sandra runs away crying. When Giulio finds her alone on a bridge, they make up. They throw the pistol from the bridge onto a moving train.

INSALATA DI RADICCHIO CON GORGONZOLA

RADICCHIO AND GORGONZOLA SALAD

In this salad, the slightly bitter taste of the radicchio blends perfectly with the heavy sweetness of the creamy dressing and the tangy flavours of the Gorgonzola.

SERVES 4

1 large head radicchio
1 tablespoon sugar
100 ml (3 ½ fl oz/scant ½ cup) grape juice
50 ml (1 ¾ fl oz/3 ½ tablespoons) balsamic vinegar
15 ml (1 tablespoon) rapeseed (canola) oil
1 teaspoon mustard
1 pear
100 g (3 ½ oz) Gorgonzola cheese
Salt
Freshly ground black pepper

IN ADDITION
1 handful unsalted pistachios, shelled

Remove the outer leaves from the radicchio, cut into quarters and remove the core. Soak the radicchio quarters in a bowl of cold water for 2 hours to remove the bitterness.

To make the vinaigrette, combine the sugar, grape juice and vinegar in a small saucepan and bring to the boil, then reduce the heat and simmer for 5 minutes until thick. Allow the liquid to cool to room temperature. Then transfer to a screw-top jar, add the oil and mustard and shake the well combined. Season to taste with salt and pepper.

Remove the radicchio from the water and dry in a salad spinner. Tear up the leaves by hand and divide among four plates. Dress the salad by drizzling with the vinaigrette.

Quarter, core and slice the pear into very thin strips. Crumble the blue cheese by hand and scatter over the salad together with the pear strips. Sprinkle with pistachios and serve.

TIP
Omit the soaking step if you prefer your radicchio bitter.

PANZANELLA

ITALIAN BREAD SALAD

Stale bread is traditionally toasted to make *panzanella*. This Mediterranean classic combines it with fresh tomato, cucumber, onion, olives and a tangy dressing, and is served as a simple starter (appetiser) or light side dish.

Cut the bread slices into thumb-size pieces. Heat the oil in a large frying pan (skillet), toast the croutons over a medium heat until golden brown and transfer to a bowl.

Peel and slice the onion into very thin rings. Drain the olives and halve lengthways. Wash the cucumber, cut in half crossways and shave into long strips with a peeler, halving again if necessary. Remove the stalks from the tomatoes, cut them in half and squeeze out the juice like a lemon (set the juice aside). Cut the flesh into small pieces and add to the croutons in the bowl together with the onion rings, cucumber strips and olives.

Peel the garlic cloves, crush through a garlic press or chop very finely and mix with the olive oil, red wine vinegar, sugar and squeezed tomato juice. Season the dressing to taste with salt and pepper. Dress and toss the salad. Leave to stand for 5 minutes, divide among four bowls, garnish with basil and serve.

SERVES 4

4 ciabatta slices, 1.5 cm (½ in) thick
5 tablespoons rapeseed (canola) oil
2 red onions
1 jar pitted green olives (400 g/14 oz/2 ⅔ cups drained)
1 organic cucumber
2 large beef tomatoes
2 garlic cloves
4 tablespoons olive oil
2 tablespoons red wine vinegar
1 pinch sugar
Salt
Freshly ground black pepper

IN ADDITION
Basil, to garnish

MINESTRONE VERDE
GREEN MINESTRONE

The most important ingredients for the most famous Italian noodle soup (*pasta in brodo*) are vegetables, tangy Parmesan and soup noodles. Thin or small pasta, such as fettuccelle or – traditionally – ditalini, are best suited to this dish.

SERVES 4

1 litre (34 fl oz/4 ¼ cups) chicken, or vegetable stock
1 piece Parmesan, with rind
200 g (7 oz/2 cups) runner (green) beans
1 small courgette (zucchini)
1 leek
150 g (5 ½ oz) soup noodles (e.g. fettuccelle)
100 g (3 ½ oz/¾ cup) frozen peas
2 tablespoons pesto (see recipe on page 71)
100 g (3 ½ oz/½ cup) fresh Parmesan shavings

Add the stock and Parmesan rind to the pot and bring to the boil. Turn off the heat and allow the stock to infuse. Clean and trim the runner beans, cut into 2–3 cm (¾–1 ¼ in) lengths and cook in boiling salted water for 5 minutes. Quarter the courgettes lengthways and thinly slice. Trim and cut the leek into thin rings.

Remove the rind from the stock and discard. Bring the stock back to the boil and cook the pasta.

Drain the runner beans and add to the stock with the courgette, leek and peas. Add the pesto just before serving. Divide the minestrone among four bowls and scatter with Parmesan shavings.

TAGLIATELLE CON LENTICCHIE MARRONI E FUNGHI

TAGLIATELLE WITH BROWN LENTILS AND MUSHROOMS

The savoury pasta sauce in this dish is reminiscent of the classic ragù. However, instead of minced meat, it is made with brown lentils. Sautéed mushrooms give the dish an irresistibly savoury umami flavour.

SERVES 4

200 g (7 oz/1 cup) brown lentils
2 shallots
4 garlic cloves
700 g (1 lb 9 oz) button mushrooms
1 bunch of parsley
500 g (1 lb 2 oz) tagliatelle
4 tablespoons olive oil
100 ml (3 ½ fl oz/scant ½ cup) white wine
200 ml (7 fl oz/scant 1 cup) cream
Freshly grated nutmeg
4 tablespoons grated freshly Parmesan
Salt
Freshly ground black pepper

Cook the lentils in water for 25 minutes until al dente. Meanwhile, peel and finely chop the shallots and garlic. Wipe the mushrooms clean, cut off the stems and thinly slice. Rinse the parsley, pat dry, pluck and coarsely chop the leaves. Cook the tagliatelle in boiling salted water until al dente according to the packet instructions.

Heat the olive oil in a large frying pan (skillet) and sauté the mushrooms. Add the shallots and garlic and sauté. Deglaze with the white wine. Add the cream and remove the pan from the heat.

Drain the lentils and add to the pan. Season the sauce with salt, pepper and nutmeg. Pour off the water from the tagliatelle, leave to drain briefly and add to the pan. Stir in half the parsley. Divide the pasta between the four plates and scatter with the Parmesan and remaining parsley.

STRACCIATELLA ALLA ROMANA

ROMAN EGG DROP SOUP

This speciality of the Lazio region is called *stracciatella* because the whisked egg, which sets in the hot meat stock, resembles shredded (*stracciato*) scrambled egg. A classic *piatto di nonna*.

Bring 750 ml (25 fl oz/3 cups) of the stock to the boil in a pot. Whisk the remaining stock with the eggs and Parmesan. Season to taste with nutmeg, salt and pepper.

Stir the egg mixture into the soup with a whisk and continue to stir briskly until the egg sets and small flakes form; this can take up to 5 minutes.

Rinse the parsley, pat dry, pluck and finely chop the leaves. Divide the soup between the four plates and sprinkle with parsley.

SERVES 4

1 litre (34 fl oz/4 ¼ cups) beef
  stock
4 eggs
5 tablespoons freshly grated
  Parmesan
Freshly grated nutmeg
Salt
Freshly ground
  black pepper
10 g (½ oz/½ cup) parsley

PASTA AL LIMONE

LEMON PASTA

This is a creamy version of the traditional lemon pasta dish. It is another example of how Italian cuisine has been able to create elegant and flavourful dishes using only a few simple but high-quality ingredients.

SERVES 4

600 g (1 lb 5 oz/6 ½ cups) pasta
  (e.g. conchiglie rigate or
  fusilli)
Grated zest and juice of
  2 organic lemons
600 ml (20 fl oz/2 ½ cups)
  cream
200 g (7 oz/generous ¾ cup)
  unsalted butter
200 g (7 oz/2 ¼ cups) freshly
  grated Parmesan
Salt
Freshly ground black pepper

IN ADDITION

2 sprigs of basil and
  1 organic lemon, to garnish

Cook the pasta according to the packet instructions. In a large pan, bring the lemon juice to the boil with half the lemon zest; it is important to have the juice boil so that the cream doesn't curdle later. Stir in the cream and butter, then simmer the sauce over a medium heat for 5 minutes. Stir in 150 g (5 ½ oz/1 ¾ cups) Parmesan until the cheese has melted and the sauce is smooth.

Pour the water off the pasta, leave to drain briefly and mix with the sauce. Season the dressing to taste with salt and pepper. Divide the pasta between the four plates and sprinkle with the remaining lemon zest and Parmesan. Serve garnished with basil leaves and lemon wedges.

SALTIMBOCCA

FRIED VEAL ESCALOPE WITH PARMA HAM AND SAGE

Although originating in the northern Italian city of Brescia, this dish is now considered a speciality of Rome. Just how good the *escalopes* (scallops) taste is clear from the name: loosely translated, *saltimbocca* means appetising food that jumps into the mouth of its own accord.

Rinse the sage leaves and pat dry. Rinse the escalopes, pat dry, place between two sheets of baking parchment and pound with a meat mallet until very thin. Lightly season both sides with some salt and pepper.

Lay three slices of Parma ham and two to three sage leaves on one side of each escalope and secure with a cocktail stick (toothpick). Heat 1 tablespoon of the butter in a frying pan (skillet) to create beurre noisette (browned butter) and fry the escalopes on the ham/sage side over a medium heat. As soon as the ham and sage leaves are lightly browned, turn over and fry the other side for 1 minute.

If you fry the escalopes one at a time in the pan, wipe with kitchen paper (paper towels) after each use. Arrange the escalopes on plates and drizzle with the remaining tablespoon of beurre noisette.

SERVES 4

10 g (½ oz) fresh sage leaves
4 thinly sliced veal escalopes (scallops) (about 150 g/5½ oz)
12 thin slices Parma ham
2 tablespoons unsalted butter
Salt
Freshly ground black pepper

TIP
Accompany with polenta, *Gnocchi alla Romana* (see recipe on page 139) or *Risotto ai Carciofi* (see recipe on page 146).

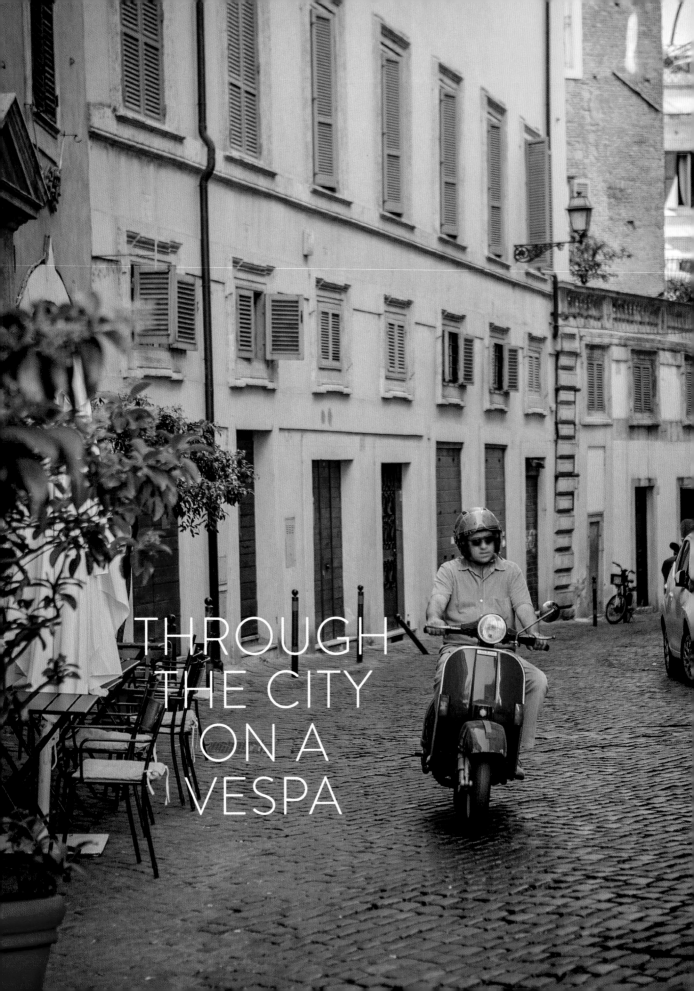

THROUGH
THE CITY
ON A
VESPA

The Vespa is as much a part of the Roman cityscape as Saint Peter's Basilica or pavement (sidewalk) cafés. A scooter is the ideal means of transport for navigating the narrow streets of the old city. It's easy to find a parking space on the side of the road, and you can even weave your way through the frequent traffic jams on your rattling two-wheeler without any problems. Over the years, riding through Rome on the back of a Vespa, past its most beautiful sights, has become an iconic image and featured in countless films.

CODA ALLA VACCINARA

OXTAIL STEW

This dish is typical of Rome's *cucina povera* – 'cooking for the poor', the name given to the food made by the humble classes – as oxtail was once considered inferior meat, alongside offal (organ meats) and cow's head. Rather than selling them, these cuts were kept by butchers (*vaccinari*) for their own use, hence the Italian description *alla vaccinara*, meaning 'in the butcher's style'.

SERVES 4

2 kg (4 lb 8 oz) oxtail, chopped into chunks and ready to cook

2 Spanish onions

2 garlic cloves

2 carrots

1 celery stalk

50 ml (1 ¾ fl oz/3 ½ tablespoons) olive oil

200 ml (7 fl oz/scant 1 cup) white wine

400 g (14 oz/1 ½ cups) tomato passata (sieved tomatoes)

600 ml (20 fl oz/2 ½ cups) beef stock

20 g (¾ oz/1 cup) parsley

Salt

Freshly ground black pepper

Rinse the oxtail pieces, pat dry and season to taste with salt. Peel and finely chop the onions, garlic and carrots. Clean and finely chop the celery.

Heat the olive oil in a pot and sear the meat on all sides. Remove the meat and sauté all the vegetables, except the celery. Deglaze with white wine and leave to simmer for 1 minute. Add the passata and stock and season with salt and pepper. Add the meat to the stock, cover with a lid and simmer for 3–4 hours. Add the celery after 2 hours of cooking. The meat is cooked when it easily comes away from the bone.

Rinse the parsley, pat dry, pluck and finely chop the leaves. Take the meat out of the pot, remove from the bones and return to the stew. Stir in the parsley. Season with salt and pepper.

TIP
Accompany with *Gnocchi alla Romana* (see recipe on page 139), potatoes or pasta.

PORCHETTA

ROLLED ROAST PORK

Pork does not play a particularly important role in Roman cuisine, aside from *salsicce* and *prosciutto*. The exception is *porchetta* – originally a suckling pig stuffed with herbs and offal (organ meats) and roasted on a spit – which is sold in speciality shops (*porchetterie*).

For the stuffing, rinse the parsley and rosemary and pat dry. Pluck and strip the leaves and grind together with the remaining ingredients in a food processor or using a pestle and mortar.

For the roast, rinse the meat, pat dry and lay skin-side up on the work surface. Using a sharp knife, score the skin with a cross pattern, making incisions 2 cm (¾ in) apart and 5 mm (¼ in) deep. Turn the meat over and spread the stuffing over the other side.

Starting on the longer side, roll up the meat very tightly, trimming off any excess edges or skin at the ends if necessary. Tie the roll with some kitchen string. Rub the skin with salt. Place the roast on a rack with the seam tucked underneath, cover and then refrigerate overnight.

The following day, wipe off the salt and rub the skin with lemon juice. Rest the meat for 30 minutes at room temperature. Preheat the oven to 115°C (240°F/gas ½). Peel the onion and slice into very thin rings. Make a bed of onion rings in the middle of a roasting tin (pan) and lay the meat on top. Roast for 4 hours. Increase the temperature to 230°C (450°F/gas 8) and cook for 20 more minutes to crisp the skin. Take the roast out of the oven and rest for at least 15 minutes. Cut into slices and serve.

TIP

Porchetta also makes an ideal filling for foccaccia.

SERVES 4

FOR THE STUFFING

1 bunch of parsley
2 sprigs of rosemary
2 teaspoons fennel seeds
1 tablespoon salt
2 teaspoons coarsely ground black pepper
1 teaspoon chilli (hot pepper) flakes

FOR THE ROAST

2.5 kg (5 lb 8 oz) pork belly, ready to cook
1 teaspoon salt
1 tablespoon lemon juice
1 Spanish onion

IN ADDITION

Kitchen string (twine)

AGNELLO ALLE ERBE CON POLENTA

HERB-MARINATED LAMB CHOPS WITH POLENTA

Lamb dishes are very popular in the Lazio region. Traditionally, chefs use suckling lamb, known as *abbacchio* in Roman cuisine, which is characterised by its particularly light and tender meat. *Agnello* refers to a lamb after weaning.

SERVES 4

FOR THE MARINADE

2 sprigs of rosemary
2 sprigs of thyme
10 g (½ oz/½ cup) parsley
3 garlic cloves
100 ml (3 ½ fl oz/scant ½ cup)
    olive oil
1 tablespoon lemon juice
Salt
Freshly ground black pepper

FOR THE POLENTA

500 ml (17 fl oz/generous 2 cups)
    milk
Freshly grated nutmeg
100 g (3 ½ oz/⅔ cup) instant
    polenta (cornmeal)
100 g (3 ½ oz/scant 1 ¼ cups)
    freshly grated Parmesan

IN ADDITION

12 trimmed lamb chops

For the marinade, rinse the herbs, pat dry, pluck and strip the leaves. Peel the garlic, combine with the herbs, olive oil and lemon juice in a blending beaker and blend to a purée with a hand-held blender. Season the marinade to taste with salt and pepper.

Rinse the lamb chops, pat dry and place in an airtight container. Add three-quarters of the marinade. Rub the chops thoroughly with the marinade, cover and refrigerate overnight.

The following day, take the meat out of the refrigerator and rest for 30 minutes. Heat a frying pan (skillet) and cook the meat on both sides over a medium heat until golden brown.

For the polenta, bring the milk and nutmeg to the boil in a saucepan and stir in the polenta. Leave to stand for 5 minutes, stirring occasionally. Stir the Parmesan into the polenta. Season with salt and pepper.

Divide the polenta among four plates and arrange three chops on top of the polenta. Drizzle with the remaining marinade and serve.

TIRAMISU

CLASSIC TIRAMISU

There is disagreement in Italy about the origin and correct way to make this most famous Italian dessert. Variants with or without eggs, alcohol or cream are common. Purists only use mascarpone, sponge fingers, sugar, egg yolks, espresso and cocoa.

Mix the espresso, rum and 80 g (2 ¾ oz/ ⅔ cup) of icing sugar in a bowl until the sugar dissolves. For the cream, beat the mascarpone with the cream and remaining 125 g (4¼ oz/1 cup) of icing sugar in a bowl with a hand-held blender until creamy. Fill a piping bag with the cream.

If necessary, trim three-quarters of the sponge fingers to the height of the glass, using a sharp knife, and soak a few at a time in the espresso and rum mixture for about 5 seconds; they should have softened a little but remain firm. Line the sides of four large glasses with the sponge pieces placed upright.

Pipe the mascarpone cream into the middle to halfway. Crumble the remaining sponge fingers and spread over the cream. Pipe the remaining cream over the top and smooth. Dust with cocoa powder through a sieve (fine-mesh strainer). Chill the tiramisu in the refrigerator for at least 6 hours before serving.

MAKES 4

250 ml (8 fl oz/1 cup) espresso or strong coffee
80 ml (2 ¾ fl oz/⅓ cup) rum
205 g (7 ¼ oz/1 ⅔ cup) icing (powdered) sugar
400 g (14 oz/1 ¾ cups) mascarpone
350 ml (12 fl oz/1 ½ cups) cream
200 g (7 oz) sponge fingers (ladyfingers)
2 tablespoons cocoa (unsweetened chocolate) powder

IN ADDITION
Piping (pastry) bag

ZABAIONE SEMIFREDDO CON AMARETTI E LAMPONI

ZABAIONE SEMIFREDDO WITH AMARETTI AND RASPBERRIES

Also known as zabaglione, this famous wine-infused mousse, made with egg yolk, sugar and Marsala, is actually served lukewarm. This semifreddo version is ideal for summer.

SERVES 4

250 ml (8 fl oz/1 cup) double (heavy) cream

3 egg yolks

60 g (2 oz/⅓ cup) sugar

75 ml (2 ½ fl oz/5 tablespoons) Marsala

150 g (5 ½ oz/1 ¼ cups) raspberries

75 g (2 ½ oz) amaretti (about 12)

IN ADDITION

20-cm (8-in) square baking tin (pan)

Whip the cream to stiff peaks, then cover and refrigerate. Whisk the egg yolks with the sugar over a bain-marie until lukewarm. Gradually stir in 50 ml (1¾ fl oz/3 ½ tablespoons) of Marsala. Transfer the mixture to a plastic bowl and leave to cool. Gently fold the whipped cream into the egg mixture.

Line the baking tin with cling film (plastic wrap) and pour in the zabaione mixture. Spread the raspberries over it. Crumble the amaretti, mix with the remaining Marsala and spread evenly over the top. Freeze for at least 6 hours.

Remove the zabaione from the freezer 20 minutes before serving and leave to thaw. Remove from the tin and cut into slices with a knife dipped in hot water.

*Il dolce far niente in
Rome: Liz strolls along
Via dell'Orso and enjoys
a good meal with her
newly friends.*

EAT PRAY LOVE

Writer Liz Gilbert (Julia Roberts) has everything she needs for a perfect New York life: a husband, a house and a successful career. Nevertheless, she is unhappy because she feels that she has lost herself and love in her life. She gets divorced and takes some time out to find herself. The film *Eat Pray Love*, which is based on Elizabeth Gilbert's best-selling memoir of the same name, tells the story of this journey across the world and to self-discovery.

The first stop Liz makes is Rome. It goes without saying that her reason for travelling to the Eternal City is for Italian cuisine. She moves into a small and decrepit apartment in Via dei Portoghesi, in the house under the famous Torre della Scimmia, the 'Monkey Tower', and experiences the city on the Tiber at its most beautiful. She drinks her morning *caffè* in a bar on the Piazza Navona, admires the Fountain of the Four Rivers, strolls through the cobbled streets of the old city, gazes out over the Eternal City at sunset from the roof terrace of Castel Sant'Angelo, eats a gelato in front of the church of Sant'Agnese in Agone and enjoys *il dolce far niente* (the sweetness of doing nothing) in the summer heat of the Italian capital. Along the way, she learns Italian from the young Giovanni and feasts her way through the kitchens of her newly found friends and the city's restaurants.

With a few extra pounds on her hips, Liz then sets off for India, where she learns to meditate in an ashram and finds inner peace. Finally, in Bali, she again encounters Ketut, a healer who during her first stay on the island had predicted that she would return and find the truth. But instead of the truth in Bali, Liz finds Felipe (Javier Bardem), who brings love back into her life after the culinary delights (eat) of Rome and the spiritual experiences (pray) of India.

SUNSET ON THE PIAZZA

The Great

BEAUTY

As the day draws to a close, the whole of Rome is bathed in warm evening light and radiates a special magic. Locals and tourists dine on the piazza, while couples in love enjoy their togetherness against this unique backdrop.

THE LAST
RAYS OF SUNLIGHT

In the early evening hours, Romans traditionally meet at a bar for an *aperitivo*. This is their way of ending the day in good company with wine, beer or an Aperol spritz. Most bars serve finger foods, such as bruschetta, olives, pizza or cheese, free of charge with a drink, and sometimes there is even a buffet featuring risotto or pasta. A summer *aperitivo* on a roof terrace in the glow of the setting sun is *il dolce far niente* Roman style.

RIGATONI ALL'AMATRICIANA

RIGATONI WITH GUANCIALE, TOMATOES AND PECORINO

A favourite of *cucina tradizionale* (traditional Italian foods), in this case a dish originating in the Lazio town of Amatrice and featured on many Roman menus.

SERVES 2

300 g (10 ½ oz/3 ⅓ cups)
   rigatoni

FOR THE SAUCE

100-g (3 ½-oz) piece guanciale
   (cured pork cheek) or
   pancetta (cured pork belly)
100 ml (3 ½ fl oz/scant ½ cup)
   white wine
400 g (14 oz/1 ⅔ cups) tinned
   chopped tomatoes
100 g (3 ½ oz/scant 1 ¼ cups)
   freshly grated pecorino
Chilli (hot pepper) flakes
Salt
Freshly ground black pepper

IN ADDITION

2 tablespoons freshly grated
   pecorino

Cook the pasta in boiling salted water until al dente according to the packet instructions.

For the sauce, cut the guanciale or pancetta into thin strips. Fry the strips in a frying pan (skillet) over a medium heat until the fat melts. Deglaze with white wine and add the tomatoes. Allow the sauce to reduce until the pasta is cooked. Stir in the pecorino right before the end of the cooking time.

Drain the pasta and add to the sauce immediately. Season to taste with salt, pepper and chilli flakes and serve scattered with pecorino.

SPAGHETTI CACIO E PEPE

SPAGHETTI WITH CHEESE AND PEPPER

This is one of the oldest and simplest Italian pasta recipes and dates from a time before the introduction of tomatoes for making *sugo* (sauce). The dish formed the base from which *rigatoni all'amatriciana* and *spaghetti alla carbonara* would develop.

Cook the spaghetti in boiling salted water until al dente according to the packet instructions. As the cooking water will be used for the sauce, it should only be lightly salted.

Mix the cheese and pepper in a metal bowl. Shortly before the spaghetti is cooked, gradually add about two ladles of cooking water to the cheese and pepper mixture while stirring briskly to fully combine the cheese with the water.

While the sauce is still quite runny, remove the spaghetti from the cooking water without draining and immediately mix well with the sauce. The sauce will thicken quickly, so dilute with a little more cooking water if necessary.

Divide the spaghetti between shallow bowls, season with coarsely ground pepper and serve immediately.

SERVES 2

300 g (10 ½ oz) spaghetti
150 g (5 ½ oz/1 ¾ cups) freshly grated pecorino
2 teaspoons coarsely ground black pepper, plus extra for serving
Salt

INSALATA DI FINOCCHI E ARANCIA

FENNEL AND ORANGE SALAD

Fennel was already popular in ancient Rome as a remedy for a wide variety of ailments. It has many recipe uses and can be braised, baked, blanched or – as in this bitter and fruity salad – simply eaten raw.

SERVES 2

1 fennel bulb (about 400 g/ 14 oz)
2 small red onions
2 oranges

FOR THE DRESSING

2–3 tablespoons runny (golden) honey
3 tablespoons hot mustard
4 tablespoons olive oil
2 tablespoons rapeseed (canola) oil
1 tablespoon (apple) cider vinegar
Salt
Coarsely ground pink pepper

For the salad, wash and quarter the fennel bulb, cut off the stalk and slice very thinly. Peel the onions, cut off the top and root and slice into very thin rings. Combine the fennel and onions in a bowl. Segment the oranges by slicing off the top and bottom, then slicing off the skin and white pith. Then release the segments by running a knife between the flesh and membrane to separate them. Collect the juice in a small bowl. Cut the orange segments into small pieces and add to the fennel and onions together with the juice.

To make the dressing, add the honey, mustard, olive oil, rapeseed oil and vinegar to a screw-top jar and season to taste with salt and pepper. Seal tightly with the lid and shake vigorously. Adjust the seasoning and pour the dressing over the salad.

Toss the salad and divide between two bowls. Sprinkle with pink pepper and serve.

ROM
ANCE

ROME, A CITY FOR LOVERS

Strolling hand in hand through narrow winding streets, kissing on the Ponte Sisto at sunset or enjoying togetherness in the shade of the trees in the gardens of Villa Borghese, Rome is full of romantic places where lovers can experience unforgettable moments. And in many of these magical places, Cupid's arrows can easily find their mark. On the Ponte Milvio, couples swear eternal love by attaching a small lock to the bridge and throwing the key into the Tiber. If you throw three coins over your shoulder into the Trevi Fountain, you will soon marry the love of your life. And, according to legend, couples who drink water together from the Fontana degli Innamorati, the lovers' fountain, remain faithful to each other forever.

GNOCCHI ALLA ROMANA

BAKED SEMOLINA GNOCCHI

Roman gnocchi aren't made from potatoes and flour; instead durum wheat semolina is used, and then they're baked in the oven with Parmesan. This dish was once always served on Thursdays.

Combine the milk with 60 g (2 oz/4 tablespoons) of the butter and the nutmeg in a saucepan and place over the heat. As soon as the butter melts, stir in the semolina. Simmer for 1 minute while stirring constantly. Transfer to a bowl and leave to cool slightly, then mix in the egg yolk and 40 g (1½ oz/½ cup) of the Parmesan and season to taste with salt and pepper.

Shape the gnocchi dough into a cylinder, place on the long edge of a sheet of baking parchment and wrap into a roll. Leave to cool.

Preheat the oven to 200°C (400°F/gas 6). Remove the baking parchment and cut the dough roll with a knife into 1-cm (½-in)-wide discs. Arrange the gnocchi discs, so they are overlapping slightly in an ovenproof dish. Melt the remaining butter and brush over the gnocchi. Sprinkle with the remaining Parmesan and bake in the oven for 15–18 minutes, until the cheese is golden.

SERVES 2

250 ml (8 fl oz/1 cup) full-fat (whole) milk

75 g (2½ oz/5 tablespoons) unsalted butter

¼ teaspoon freshly grated nutmeg

125 g (4 ½ oz/1 cup) semolina

1 egg yolk

100 g (3 ½ oz/scant 1 ¼ cups) freshly grated Parmesan

Salt

Freshly ground black pepper

IN ADDITION

Ovenproof dish, 20 cm (8 in) in diameter

TIP

These gnocchi make a great starter (appetiser) and an ideal accompaniment for *Pollo alla Romana* (see recipe on page 154).

SPAGHETTI ALLA CARBONARA

SPAGHETTI WITH EGG AND GUANCIALE

Although this typical Roman dish is made from a few very simple ingredients, it isn't quite so easy to prepare. The perfect result has the spaghetti finely coated in the egg and pecorino sauce.

SERVES 2

300 g (10 ½ oz) spaghetti
100 g (3 ½ oz) guanciale,
 or pancetta, cut into strips
100 g (3 ½ oz/scant 1 ¼ cups)
 freshly grated pecorino
4 egg yolks
Salt
Freshly ground
 black pepper

Cook the spaghetti in boiling salted water until al dente according to the packet instructions. As the cooking water will be used for the sauce, it should only be lightly salted.

Fry the guanciale strips in a frying pan (skillet) over a medium heat until golden brown. In a large metal bowl, whisk the pecorino with the egg yolks until combined. Just before the spaghetti is cooked, stir two ladles of cooking water into the egg and cheese mixture with a whisk.

Remove the spaghetti from the cooking water without draining and immediately mix with the sauce. Although the sauce may still be a little runny at first, the pasta will absorb a lot of the liquid. Stir in the guanciale strips and season to taste with salt and pepper. Serve immediately.

RISOTTO ALLE VONGOLE E LIMONE

RISOTTO WITH CLAMS AND LEMON

Rome, and the Lazio region in general, is better known for its wide variety of pasta dishes than for rice. Nonetheless, this clam risotto is simple and wonderfully light, yet refined and bursting with flavour.

Brush the clams under cold running water. Discard any open ones. Peel and finely chop the onion. Finely chop the anchovy fillets.

Bring 500 ml (17 fl oz/generous 2 cups) of the fish stock to the boil in a saucepan. Heat the olive oil in a second pan and sauté the onion. Add the rice and anchovies and sauté briefly. Deglaze with the white wine and allow the liquid to reduce for 1 minute. Gradually ladle in the hot stock. Always allow the liquid to reduce first before adding the next ladle of stock; meanwhile, continue to simmer the stock in the pan over a low heat. The risotto is ready when the rice is cooked but firm to the bite and has absorbed all the stock; this can take about 20 minutes.

Shortly before the risotto is cooked, bring the remaining fish stock to the boil in a pan. Add the clams, cover with a lid and simmer for 8 minutes.

Stir the lemon zest and Parmesan into the finished risotto. Season to taste with salt and pepper. Rinse the lemon thyme, pat dry and pluck the leaves. Divide the risotto between the two plates and top with the mussels. Garnish with lemon thyme.

SERVES 2

500 g (1 lb 2 oz) Venus clams
1 Spanish onion
2 anchovy fillets
1 litre (34 fl oz/4 ¼ cups) fish stock
2 tablespoons olive oil
180 g (6 ¼ oz/scant 1 cup) risotto rice
50 ml (1 ¾ fl oz/3 ½ tablespoons) white wine
Zest of ½ organic lemon
50 g (1 ¾ oz/⅔ cup) freshly grated Parmesan
2 sprigs of lemon thyme
Salt
Freshly ground black pepper

RISOTTO AI CARCIOFI

RISOTTO WITH ARTICHOKES

Artichokes are one of the main ingredients in Roman cuisine. They can be found at the city's markets starting in March. And there is even a special variety, the *Carciofo Romanesco*, which is grown around Rome.

SERVES 2

180 g (6 ¼ oz) artichoke hearts
   (from a jar)
1 Spanish onion
6 large sage leaves
500 ml (17 fl oz/generous 2
   cups) vegetable stock
2 tablespoons olive oil
180 g (6 ¼ oz/scant 1 cup)
   risotto rice
50 ml (1 ¾ fl oz/3 ½
   tablespoons) white wine
50 g (1 ¾ oz/⅔ cup) freshly
   grated Parmesan
Zest of 1 organic lemon
Salt
Freshly ground black pepper

Drain and quarter the artichoke hearts. Peel and finely chop the onion. Rinse the sage leaves and pat dry.

Bring the stock to the boil in a saucepan. Heat the oil in a second pan and fry the sage leaves over a medium heat until golden. Remove the leaves, add the onion and sauté in the same oil. Add the rice and sauté briefly. Deglaze with the white wine and allow the liquid to reduce a little. Gradually ladle in the hot stock. Always allow the liquid to reduce first before adding the next ladle of stock; meanwhile, continue to simmer the stock in the pan over a low heat. The risotto is ready when the rice is cooked but firm to the bite and has absorbed all the stock; this can take about 20 minutes.

Stir the Parmesan and lemon zest into the finished risotto. Season to taste with salt and pepper. Stir in half of the artichokes and heat gently. Divide the risotto between the two plates and arrange the remaining artichokes on top. Garnish with the fried sage leaves and serve hot.

PESCE AL FORNO CON POMODORI, OLIVE E CAPPERI

BAKED FISH WITH TOMATOES, OLIVES AND CAPERS

The combination of tomatoes, olives and capers is popular in the cuisines of many Italian regions. In Rome, it is used in *pasta alla puttanesca* or as an accompaniment for fish.

Rinse the sole fillet and pat dry, then halve lengthways and position each half in the middle of doubled sheets of baking parchment. Peel and finely slice the garlic. Rinse the thyme and pat dry. Rinse the lemon in hot water, pat dry and cut into thin slices. Halve the olives.

Preheat the oven to 175°C (350°F/gas 4). Heat the oil in a frying pan (skillet) and sauté the tomatoes over a low heat until soft. Add the garlic and thyme and sauté until the garlic is lightly coloured. Cover the fish pieces with the garlic, tomatoes and thyme. Then arrange the lemon slices, olive halves and capers on top. Season the fish to taste with salt and pepper and drizzle with the wine.

Wrap the parchment around the fish into parcels to hold in the steam. Staple them closed if necessary. Place the parcels on a baking sheet and bake for 25–30 minutes.

TIP
This dish can be accompanied with ciabatta or a simple risotto.

SERVES 2

1 ready-to-cook sole fillet (about 600 g/1 lb 5 oz)
4 garlic cloves
4 sprigs of thyme
1 organic lemon
50 g (1 ¾ oz/⅓ cup) pitted green olives
3 tablespoons olive oil
200 g (7 oz/1 ⅓ cups) cherry tomatoes
20 g (¾ oz/2 ½ tablespoons) capers
4 tablespoons white wine
Salt
Freshly ground black pepper

IN ADDITION
4 sheets baking parchment

Viva la notte

When night falls in Rome and the hustle and bustle of the day subsides, the city is at its most enchanting. Against the dark night sky, the ancient buildings are illuminated by the warm glow of floodlights, creating a magical backdrop for a stroll through empty streets and across deserted squares, such as the Piazza del Popolo. Sights that are normally crowded with tourists during the day can now be admired serenely, and some only reveal their true beauty in the darkness.

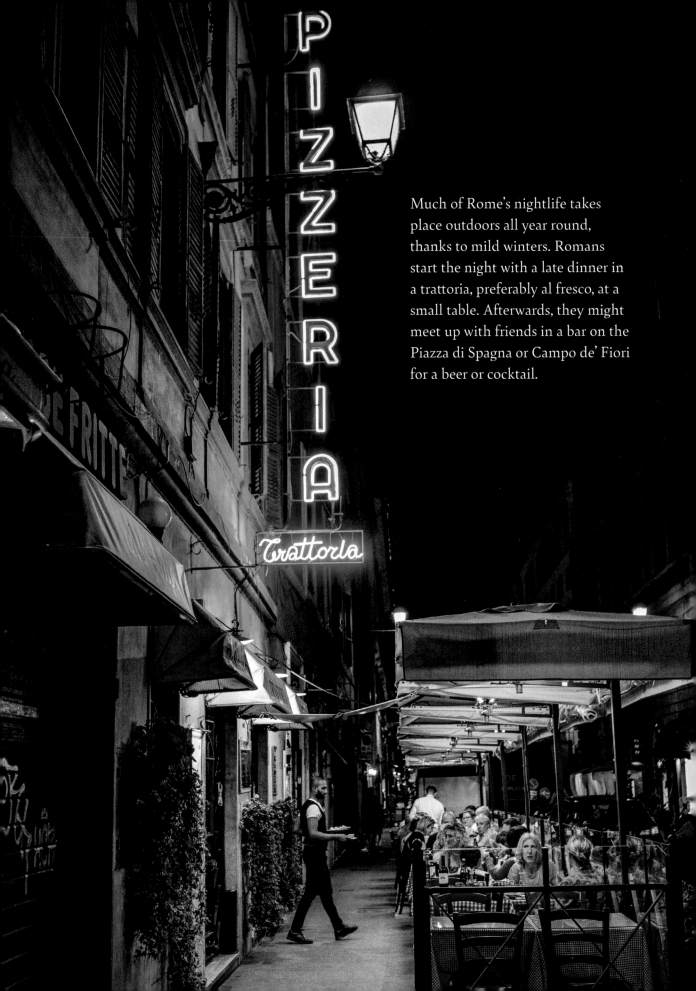

Much of Rome's nightlife takes place outdoors all year round, thanks to mild winters. Romans start the night with a late dinner in a trattoria, preferably al fresco, at a small table. Afterwards, they might meet up with friends in a bar on the Piazza di Spagna or Campo de' Fiori for a beer or cocktail.

POLLO ALLA ROMANA

CHICKEN WITH PEPPERS AND TOMATOES

This typical Roman dish is traditionally served on *Ferragosto*, as the 15 August, or Feast of the Assumption, is known. It can also be enjoyed cold on hot days.

SERVES 2

2 chicken breasts (about
   200 g/7 oz)
1 red and 1 yellow
   (bell) pepper
2 vine-ripened tomatoes
½ Spanish onion
3 garlic cloves
2 tablespoons butter
100 ml (3 ½ fl oz/scant ½ cup)
   chicken stock
1 tablespoon chilli (hot pepper)
   flakes
1 teaspoon dried marjoram
3 tablespoons olive oil
Salt
Freshly ground
   black pepper

IN ADDITION
Fresh marjoram, to
   garnish

Rinse the chicken breasts, pat dry and season with salt on both sides. Peel, deseed and slice the peppers into thin strips. Remove the stalks from the tomatoes and cut them into large chunks. Peel and roughly chop the onion and garlic.

Heat the butter in a saucepan and sauté the onion, garlic and half the yellow pepper strips. Add the tomatoes and leave to simmer briefly. Add the chicken stock and then purée the mixture with a hand-held blender to a smooth sauce. Add the chilli flakes and marjoram, season to taste with salt and pepper, cover with a lid and simmer for 5 minutes.

Heat 2 tablespoons of the olive oil in a large frying pan (skillet) and fry the chicken on both sides over a low heat until golden brown. Remove, heat the remaining olive oil in the pan and sauté the remaining pepper strips. Spoon the sauce onto plates and arrange the meat and pepper strips on top.

TIP
The chicken can be accompanied with ciabatta, pasta or potatoes.

FICHI MARINATI CON FORMAGGIO

CHEESE-STUFFED MARINATED FIGS

In Italian cuisine, figs are often paired with something savoury, such as Parma ham, or a salty cheese, such as pecorino, Parmesan or Gorgonzola. Italians refer to these dishes as *agrodolce* (sweet and sour).

Wash the figs and remove the stalks. Cut a 2-cm (¾-in)-deep cross into the open side with a knife. Remove the stems from the redcurrants. Purée the redcurrants in a food processor and filter through a sieve (fine-mesh strainer) into a small saucepan. Add the red wine vinegar and 200 ml (7 fl oz/scant 1 cup) of red wine and bring to the boil.

Mix the cornflour with the remaining red wine until smooth and add to the hot liquid. Simmer for 1 minute while stirring constantly, then stir in the honey. Transfer the marinade to a bowl and leave to cool for 30 minutes. Add the figs to the marinade, cover and marinate in the refrigerator for at least 4 hours or overnight.

Take the cheese and figs out of the refrigerator 1 hour before serving. Cut the cheese into very thin slices or crumble, depending on the variety. Remove the figs from the marinade and stuff with the cheese through the cross opening. Widen the opening a little more if necessary to fit the cheese.

SERVES 2

6 figs
250 g (9 oz/1 ¼ cups)
    redcurrants
1 tablespoon red wine vinegar
250 ml (8 fl oz/1 cup) red wine
1 teaspoon cornflour
    (cornstarch)
1 tablespoon honey
100 g (3 ½ oz) cheese (e.g.
    pecorino or Gorgonzola)

TIP

Instead of this savoury version, the figs can also be prepared as a sweet dessert. Simply add a little more honey to the marinade and stuff with ricotta.

PANNA COTTA CON AMARENE

PANNA COTTA WITH AMARENA CHERRIES

Panna cotta is one of the most tempting *dolci* in Italian cuisine. Together with the Amarena cherries in syrup prepared at home, this sweet treat is not to be missed.

SERVES 2

FOR THE PANNA COTTA

3 gelatine leaves (sheets)

300 ml (10 fl oz/1 ¼ cups) double (heavy) cream

100 ml (3 ½ fl oz/scant ½ cup) full-fat (whole) milk

50 g (1 ¾ oz/¼ cup) sugar

Seeds from ½ vanilla pod (bean)

FOR THE AMARENA CHERRIES IN SYRUP

500 g (1 lb 2 oz/3 ¼ cups) frozen Amarena cherries, or sour cherries

110 g (4 oz/generous ½ cup) sugar

1 teaspoon fresh lemon juice

50 ml (1 ¾ fl oz/3 ½ tablespoons) amaretto

Bitter almond flavouring (optional)

For the panna cotta, soak the gelatine in cold water for 5 minutes. Heat the cream, milk, sugar and vanilla seeds in a saucepan. Squeeze the gelatine well to drain and add to the vanilla cream, stirring to dissolve completely. Pour the panna cotta mixture into glasses and refrigerate for 6 hours.

For the Amarena cherries in syrup, defrost the cherries for 30 minutes. In a saucepan, simmer the cherries with the sugar and lemon juice over a medium heat for 15 minutes. Add the amaretto and a few drops of bitter almond flavouring (if using) and cook the cherries for 15 more minutes, until the liquid is syrupy. Transfer to a bowl and leave to cool, then cover and refrigerate.

Remove the panna cotta from the refrigerator. Run a knife around the sides of the glasses and carefully turn out each panna cotta onto a small plate, or serve them in the glasses. Serve with the Amarena cherries in syrup.

TIP

Instead of making your own syrup with frozen cherries, you can use Amarena cherries in syrup from a jar (350 g/12 oz/2 cups drained weight). However, these will have less crunch.

THE BEST
ICE CREAM
IN THE CITY

If you ask Romans for the best ice cream in the city, you will receive many different recommendations. One of the reasons for this is that there is a higher density of ice cream parlours in Rome than in almost any other city. Eating ice cream, or gelato as the local variety is known, is as much a part of Rome as pasta, pizza, wine or espresso.

Many long-established ice cream parlours make their gelato fresh every day according to a traditional recipe. Some offer over 100 different flavours. In addition to classic flavours such as *cioccolato*, *pistacchio* and *fragola*, you will also find more unusual creations such as *peperoncino*, Gorgonzola and celery, or exotic combinations such as Gorgonzola with chocolate or Taleggio cheese with a beer reduction and pecan nuts. Even fans of vegan, whole food or raw food diets can have their fill at some Roman ice cream parlours that offer special recipes. On request, the gelato can often be dipped in melted chocolate or topped either with whipped cream or zabaglione at no extra charge.

One of the city's most famous *gelaterie* is Giolitti, near the Pantheon, while the Palazzo del Freddo Giovanni Fassi, founded in 1880, is one of the oldest. Some ice cream parlours, such as Otaleg and Gelateria dei Gracchi, have even made it into the Italian gourmet guide *Gambero Rosso* with their creations. If you are looking for the most delicious gelato in town, look out for ice cream parlours with long queues of locals. The wait is often rewarded with the perfect ice cream treat.

SORBETTO AL LIMONE

LEMON SORBET

Lemon sorbet, particularly when combined with limoncello, prosecco or vodka, is a classic. It can be enjoyed as a dessert without alcohol, and it tastes just as good.

In a saucepan, make a syrup by combining the sugar, water, lemon zest and limoncello, (if using), and bring to the boil until the sugar dissolves. Strain the liquid through a fine-mesh sieve (strainer) into a bowl and leave to cool.

Stir the fresh lemon juice into the syrup, pour into the ice cream maker and churn for about 20 minutes. Alternatively, put the mixture into a freezer-save container, cover with a lid and freeze for 6 hours, stirring from time to time.

To serve, dip an ice cream scoop in hot water and scoop out balls.

SERVES 2

200 g (7 oz/1 cup) sugar
225 ml (7½ fl oz/scant 1 cup)
  water
Zest of 1 organic lemon
2 tablespoons limoncello
  (optional)
200 ml (7 fl oz/scant 1 cup)
  freshly squeezed
  lemon juice

IN ADDITION
Ice cream maker

THE GREAT BEAUTY

The life of failed writer Jep Gambardella (Toni Servillo) consists of little more than lavish parties, fine restaurants, Botox parties, beautiful women and sex. While he was feted 40 years earlier for his first – and so far only – novel, he now earns his living as a journalist writing cynical reviews of modern art. On his rooftop terrace, with its spectacular view of the Colosseum at sunset, he and his friends from sophisticated Roman society pass the time by gossiping over a gin and tonic. People cultivate the pretence of beauty and are wary of exposing the illusion on which their lives are built. Because anyone who looks behind the shiny facade will be staring into an abyss of self-deception, failure and despair.

Jep is tired of this life. It's his 65th birthday and he feels old. When he discovers that his first great love, who had left him 35 years before and married someone else, has died, he recognises his own transience. Suddenly confronted with death, he has to admit that he has wasted 40 years of his life in the Eternal City: 'This is my life … and it's nothing.' It's a life in which time has stood still, like in the Campo Verano cemetery or in the Roman palazzi with their unapproachable sculptures and paintings, into which Jep escorts his lover Ramona (Sabrina Ferilli) one night, and which the 2013 film *The Great Beauty* (original Italian title *La Grande Belleza*) shows in all its incomprehensible glory. It's a life which, like the line dance at one of the parties, though turning and changing direction, leads nowhere.

Jep realises that this endless party was his way of trying to distract himself from the pain of losing his first great love. And in the end, he also realises why he hasn't written another novel in all these years. He was always in search of great beauty, a moment of silence and sensitivity, which he could never find amid all the noise, chatter and inanities of Rome.

GLOSSARY OF ITALIAN CULINARY TERMS

aglio · Garlic
agnello · Lamb
agrodolce · Sweet and sour
al dente · Firm to the bite
al taglio · By the slice
albicocca · Apricot
amaretti · Almond macaroons
amarene · Amarena cherries
anguria · Watermelon
antipasti · Starters (appetisers) or hors d'oeuvres
aperitivo · Pre-dinner drink
arancia · Orange
Ascolana Tenera · A variety of olive native to the Ascoli Piceno region asparagi · Asparagus

bignè · Choux bun
bomboloni · Italian doughnuts
bruschetta · Toasted white bread rubbed with garlic and served with oil and tomato

cacio · Cheese; cacio is an old term for *formaggio*
caffè · Espresso
calamari fritti · Deep-fried calamari (squid) rings
cantuccini · Almond biscuits
capperi · Capers
carciofi · Artichokes
cena in famiglia · Family dinner
ciliegia · Cherry
cioccolato · Chocolate
cornetto · Croissant
crostata · Tart
cucina povera · Cooking for the poor
cucina tradizionale · Traditional cuisine

della nonna · Grandmother's prepared food
dolce · Dessert
dolce · Sweet
dolci · Sweet food

erbe · Herbs

fagiolo · Bean
fichi · Figs

finocchio · Fennel
focaccia · Italian flatbread
frittata · Omelette
funghi · Mushrooms

gelato · Ice cream
gnocchi · Egg-shaped, dumplings made with potato or durum wheat semolina

insalata · Salad
involtini · Rolls

lamponi · Raspberries
lenticchie marroni · Brown lentils
limoncello · Lemon liqueur
limone · Lemon

mandorle amare · Bitter almonds
maritozzi · Sweet buns
mascarpone · Mild and thick fresh cheese made with double (heavy) cream
melanzana · Aubergine (eggplant)
minestrone · Vegetable (and noodle) soup
mortazza · Wafer-thin mortadella slice
mozzarella di bufala · Buffalo mozzarella

olio d'oliva · Olive oil
oliva · Olive

pane · Bread
panini · Small sandwiches filled with cheese and/or sausage
panna cotta · Gelatine-set cream dessert
panzanella · Italian bread salad
parmigiano · Parmesan
pasta in brodo · Noodle soup
pasticciere · Pastry chef
patate · Potatoes
pepe · Pepper
pesce al forno · Baked fish
pinoli · Pine nuts
pinsa · Focaccia-like flatbread, resembling a pizza but prepared differently

pistacchio · Pistachio
pizza bianca · White pizza, prepared without tomato sauce
polenta · Coarsely ground corn (cornmeal)
pollo · Chicken
pomodoro · Tomato
porchetta · A suckling pig stuffed with herbs and offal (organ meat) and roasted on a spit
primo piatto · First course, starter (appetiser)
prosciutto · Dry-cured ham
prosciutto di Parma · Parma ham

ragù · Minced (ground) meat sauce
ricotta · Whey cheese, similar to cottage cheese
rosmarino · Rosemary

sale · Salt
saltimbocca · Veal escalope (scallop) with ham and sage
salsiccia · Fresh, chunky sausage
secondo piatto · Second course, main course
semifreddo · Semi-frozen
sorbetto · Sorbet
sugo · Sauce
supplì · Rice balls, filled rice croquettes (e.g. with minced/ground beef)

torta · Tart

vaccinaro · Butcher
vongole · Clams

zabaione · Zabaglione, wine-infused mousse

RECIPE INDEX

INGREDIENTS INDEX

INGREDIENTS INDEX

INGREDIENTS INDEX

LISA NIESCHLAG

... is a designer, cookery book author and photographer.

Her photography whets the appetite of many readers for more, particularly because of her tasteful styling and staging. Food is Lisa's creative and culinary cosmos. In addition to her food photography, Lisa's atmospheric portrayal of Rome shows her very personal view of the Eternal City.

Lisa runs the popular Food blog Liz & Friends.

www.lizandfriends.de

AUTHORS

LARS WENTRUP

... is an all-rounder: designer, illustrator, gourmet and food tester. And he loves books.

Inspired by the creative food styling and the impressive imagery, Lars creates the perfect platform and captures their wonderful flavour – in every respect – on paper.

Lars and Lisa have been jointly managing a communication design agency in Münster, Germany, since 2001.

www.nieschlag-wentrup.de

GRAZIE

Armed with a camera and wearing our sunhats, we wandered Rome in search of photo opportunities: sunset with a view of the city from the Pincio Terrace, commotion and activity at the Trevi Fountain, scorching heat at the Roman Forum, and shady backstreets away from the tourist hotspots – there's never a lack of opportunity in Rome. Fortunately, we were able to build up our strength in some of the many restaurants and espresso bars between places and experience Rome's culinary delights. We would like to say *molte grazie* to our team Tina Ballerstaedt and Niklas Birkemeyer for holding down the fort at our agency in the meantime.

We would also like to thank Verena Poppen for the culinary collaboration and Louisa Duckwitz, Mareike Bartholomäus and Franziska Grünewald for their great support for our project. We thank Carlotta Pape, Friederike Wentrup and Susan Nieschlag for their invaluable assistance with cooking on set. We can only create books like these with the help of such a good team.

Thank you, dear Hölker Verlag. We share a great passion for beautiful books. Thank you, dear Jasmin, for the inspiration to create this book!

Many thanks also to our cooperative partners Motel a Miio and Botz.

This edition published in 2024 by Hardie Grant Books, an imprint of Hardie Grant Publishing.

Original edition © 2023 Hölker Verlag
a part of Coppenrath Verlag GmbH & Co. KG, Hafenweg 30, 48155 Münster, Germany.
Original title: Verliebt in Roma. Rezepte und Geschichten
(ISBN 978-3-88117-298-1)

Hardie Grant Books (London)
5th & 6th Floors
52–54 Southwark Street
London SE1 1UN

Hardie Grant Books (Melbourne)
Building 1, 658 Church Street
Richmond, Victoria 3121
hardiegrantbooks.com

In Love with Rome
ISBN: 9781784886936
10 9 8 7 6 5 4 3 2 1

Idea and concept:
Lisa Nieschlag und Lars Wentrup
Hölker Verlag
Authors:
Lisa Nieschlag und Lars Wentrup
Layout and type:
Nieschlag + Wentrup
communication design agency
www.nieschlag-wentrup.de

Illustration
Lars Wentrup
Styling, food and Rome photography:
Lisa Nieschlag
www.lisanieschlag.de
Other photographs:
P. 13: picture alliance / United Archives | United Archives / kpa Publicity picture alliance / Farabola/Leemage | © Farabola/Leemage. P. 41: picture alliance / Sammlung Richter | Sammlung Richter. P. 95 & P. 124 (kl. Bild): picture alliance. P. 124 (gr. Bild): picture alliance / Everett Collection | © Columbia Pictures / Courtesy Everett Collection
Additional texts:
Dr. Christine Schlitt
Recipe development:
Verena Poppen
Proofreading:
Dr. Christine Schlitt
Editing:
Mareike Bartholomäus, www.hafentexterei.de
Anna Louisa Duckwitz
Franziska Grünewald
Assistance:
Friederike Wentrup
Carlotta Pape
Production:
Dana Günther
Lithography:
FSM Premedia GmbH & Co. KG, Münster
We would like to thank Motel a Miio for providing the props.

Publishing Director: Kajal Mistry
Typesetting: David Meikle
Translation: Cillero & de Motta
Proofreader: Caroline West
Production controller: Martina Georgieva
Colour reproduction by p2d
Printed and bound in China by Leo Paper Products Ltd.

MIX
Paper | Supporting responsible forestry
FSC
www.fsc.org
FSC™ C020056